PATTERNS

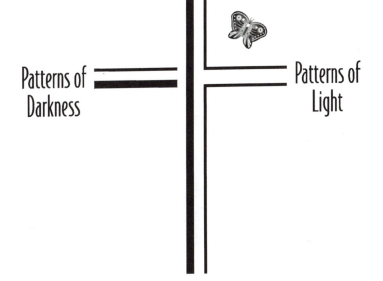

Patterns of Darkness

Patterns of Light

A true story of a life almost destroyed by
alcoholism & prescription drug addiction and the
miraculous healing that changed her forever

PATTERNS

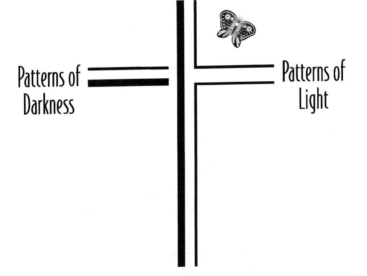

Patterns of
Darkness

Patterns of
Light

A true story of a life almost destroyed by
alcoholism & prescription drug addiction and the
miraculous healing that changed her forever

Karen Fairweather Kemp

WINEPRESS WP PUBLISHING

Printed in the United States of America.

Packaged by WinePress Publishing, PO Box 428, Enumclaw, WA 98022. The views expressed or implied in this work do not necessarily reflect those of WinePress Publishing. The author is ultimately responsible for the design, content, and editorial accuracy of this work.

ISBN 1-57921-423-1
Library of Congress Catalog Card Number: 2001096399

*D*edication

Dedicated to the memory of my mother, Ruth; to Grandma Lena, Mama Hon and Uncle Ernie, Aunt Alice and Uncle Porter, who held me and gave me years of laughter; to Sumner, who recently lost the battle; to the memory of Dr. Norman V. Peale, whose personal letters of encouragement to write remain a treasure—and to you in need of hope . . .

$\mathcal{A}$cknowledgements

With appreciation and thanks from my heart to my husband of forty-eight years, Bill, for his unconditional love and his technical help in producing Patterns. For the precious gift of my children Julie, Barbara, and David. To Barbara Kenworthy Garfield for hanging in there with me for over sixty-two years and loving me like a sister. To Barbara Schlauch, editor-in-chief, for her insight, valuable time and spirited encouragement. To Verla Boehme for her equally superb editing, her confidence in me and her patience. For all the prayers that Patterns will make a difference in someone's life and that God will be honored.

*T*able of Contents

"Gate to 'Peters Burrow'"

*T*HE GATE OF REFLECTION

1

*T*he memory of my mother's struggles—alcoholism, the tragedy of the fire and the death and the multiple losses—stirred deeply in my mind. I had once searched through charcoal rubble and ashes for possessions, for memoirs—for something to grasp out of an eerie scene—and now years later, I felt a need to search for roots and for understanding of where she had come from and what I had been given.

My forever friend Barbara had invited me to her home on the East Coast for an adventure throughout New England with the primary goal of seeing my birthplace. We were driving through the White Mountains of New Hampshire in early October toward that long-awaited dream of mine—to see through the eyes of an adult the actual place where my mother had retreated fifty-five years earlier.

Her name was Ruth, and after marrying a man named Gil back in their home state of Wisconsin in 1929, and after becoming pregnant with me, she and my father separated. Struggling with what she should do, she boarded a train for New Hampshire and the small village of Peterborough where a close friend had relocated. And now I would see at last where my mother had lived, the streets she walked, the hills she climbed, the kind of people she knew, and where I was born on a cold March early morning.

The day began with a frost that crisped the air and sugared the hills of autumn harvest. The sun shone over the Grand Monadnock Mountain and the Contoocook River meandered under the old stone bridge that we crossed into the village of "Peter's Burrow" as it was known until chartered in 1739. Red brick buildings and white steeples stood solid and graceful against the cerulean blue sky—a beautiful morning in Peterborough, and I felt like a foreigner with a piece of nostalgia in my pocket. I was eager to see 22 Winter Street. We drove through the freedom-loving Yankee town and up the winding hill to the left. On a quiet neighborhood street with houses placed far apart, there sat a charming, yet simple, French country style home— friendly and distinctive. There was a view of the hills with their soft beginning of reds and golds, and the town of about five thousand inhabitants below. The friends my mother had stayed with still lived there but were not at home. We peeked in the cross-paned windows and followed the well-kept green lawn around to the back, and I imagined the sunrise over the hills beyond as my mother might have seen it from her second story window that I chose for her. As I considered the loneliness and anticipation she must have felt, I was grateful for the gentle strength and loving security that I knew she had received here. Gentleness and joy were to become alien to her in life.

"Just think, you're walking where your mother walked," Barbara said as we ventured down the tree-laden street for a few minutes before getting in her Audi to drive back to the Village Green. White columns, red brick historic architecture, green hedges and sugar maples along the narrow scrubbed streets contributed to the aristocratic graciousness in this seemingly isolated flag-waving town—*Our Town*, the actual setting in the early thirties for Thornton Wilder's Pulitzer Prize-winning play. We entered the two-story Town Hall, with its central winding staircase and white framed windows letting in the sunshine all the way up, and found where I could get a copy of my birth certificate that read, "Karin Ann Schmidling—March 17, 1932." I knew I loved being born in Peterborough in the "Granite State" of New Hampshire. We discovered the brick Federalist Building that houses one of the most active historical societies in New Hampshire and the library that reportedly is the first tax-supported free public library in the world. We learned that fine classical music is an integral part of the lives of these people, and the excellence of the concerts held here is recognized throughout New England. We walked into shops that sold homemade woolens, books, sporting goods—all that gave away the lifestyle for the coming winter months in this vigorous part of the country.

Back in the car, Barbara drove on to the "gate" of Peterborough, the gray stone bridge that arched over blue water and rocky shores. In my heart I said goodbye, and we continued around the golden tree-lined curves to the outskirts of town to see the dark red brick hospital. I recalled my mother telling me years later how she had crawled along the hospital corridors in agonizing labor. I tried to picture her now and felt very sad that she had to go through all that pain without her husband. We viewed the sprawled out building from the parking lot and then drove on—it was time to absorb and reflect on the beautiful adventure of the day—time to tell my friend what happened in the lives of Ruth and Karin after March 17 of '32.

*I*N THE ARMS OF TRUTH

2

*W*hen I was about four months old and living on Winter Street, my father called from Chicago begging my mother to return with me in tow. We boarded the train and three days later pulled into Union Station with hope and anticipation, searching the crowds. He wasn't there. What kind of man was this? The "most brilliant man to graduate from Marquette University" not too many years earlier—a full-blooded German who was one of the inventors of the television tube—where was his heart, his sense of family commitment—why was his word not good? We were abandoned on a hot summer day without a home in a big, noisy city. Heartbroken, my mother took me to the YWCA where we stayed overnight, then took another train for Oshkosh, Wisconsin, where her older sister lived. Aunt Alice, Uncle Porter and my three cousins were my new care givers and made me a part of their family for the next year while my mother returned to Chicago for a well-paying job as a legal secretary in the Palmolive Building. We were to live apart for the next few years.

When my uncle's asthma forced their move to southern California, I was taken to the La Crosse home of the younger sister, my aunt Helen—Mama Hon as I was to call her—and Uncle Ernie, two cousins and Grandma Lena, the rest of the Norwegian side of my family. Lena's parents, Ingaborg and Hans Jensen had come to America from Bergen. There were so many Jensens aboard ship who had plans to settle in Wisconsin that several families decided to change their names. Ingaborg and Hans became the Toppens and built their log cabin home in Galesville. It was there, in 1873, that my grandmother was born. Many years later, Lena was to marry Nicholas Ray Kienzle, whose family made watches in Christiania (now Oslo), Norway. Grandfather Nick owned a cement factory in Galesville and built streets and sidewalks. He also made bricks and built the Lutheran Church in that small town. The family belonged to the Trinity Lutheran Church, a Zion Lutheran congregation where my mother was baptized and a member. Eventually, when her father joined the Masonic Lodge and because Lutherans didn't accept masons for membership, the Kienzles changed to the Congregational Church. They maintained that membership after their move to La Crosse several years later. It was in La Crosse that, as a toddler, I was moved into their home.

The large, old brick and clapboard house at 216 West Avenue North is where I lived for the next four years. We had two parlors, one with a piano and fainting floral tapestry couch, the other with a fireplace, in front of which Mama Hon had us rolling on the floor in gales of laughter as she told her funny stories. The dining room was quite large and also had a fireplace which was centered between two floor-to-ceiling windows. The big mahogany table was a favorite place to sit with Grandma Kienzle for a midmorning sweet roll. Our daily noon gathering place was at that table.

Uncle Ernie always said a blessing before the meal. Grandma sat at the other end of the table, Mama Hon next to her and my oldest cousin next to her dad. Gretchen and I sat on the other side, looking across at Ruthie peeling off her nail polish, flakes falling into our standard fare of Spanish Rice, and my uncle would grimace.

Hud in the story ....'
Katie told Things Her.

The dining room was also where Grandma fitted us with the lavender and white pinafores she made and said "ya" and "goot" a thousand times, and where Uncle Ernie had his Friday night poker parties. The pale green kitchen was small, though it had room for the very best apple pies, sugar cookies and Norwegian lefsa to be prepared. Behind the kitchen lived one of our roomers. We had a large screened-in front porch with gray-green wicker furniture where we sat during the summer months—after going to the corner drugstore with Uncle Ernie for blackberry ice cream cones. The dark gray basement was where Grandma did the family laundry with an old tub and wringer and where my uncle stoked the fiery hot black coal furnace and cleaned his slimy fish from the Mississippi River.

Up the winding staircase, off the front parlor, where I loved to sit with my stuffed bear Honey and listen to anything, were bedrooms for my aunt and uncle, my younger cousin Gretchen and the one that Grandma shared with me. It was in that big fluffy bed, surrounded by cabbage rose wallpaper, that I could snuggle in with her as she protected me from the booming thunderstorms and where she comforted me because of bad dreams or loneliness for my mother, and it was where, night after night, she said and taught me The Lord's Prayer.

There were roomers on that floor too. "Aunt" Grace was a spinster school teacher who lived with her elderly white-haired mother, "Grandma" Ogden, who had a wooden leg. Gretchen and I ventured down the hallway each morning to watch Grandma Ogden clean off her short stump, just above the knee, with cotton and spirits. She then carefully attached her wooden leg with straps as she told us how the Indians had shot off her leg with a bow and arrow when she was a young woman.

Just before the entrance to their quarters was the door to another special place for us. At the top of the steep stairs in the attic was an extra wooden leg that Gretchen and I would attempt to wear and hobble around on up there in the middle of the night. Bats got in the attic through the window crevices and we had to dive under the sheets of the feather bed, feathers flying toward the high crossbeams. A large trunk filled with old clothes and fancy beads that we could dress up in was on the right of the stairway. Straight ahead was the front dormer room that my teenage cousin claimed as her own—where she slept, did her homework, polished her nails and dreamed of Andy. In the back of our home was the rented Honeymoon Cottage, and Ruthie could hardly wait to use it.

I was never aware of how utterly exhausted Mama Hon must have been each night. She was a fastidious housekeeper and maintained the large old house by herself, and she was an excellent cook. She managed the four steady roomers plus the frequent honeymooners in addition to her own family. Mama Hon knit our beautiful blue and white Norwegian sweaters with hats to match, and as a storyteller, she caused her own laughter, which came from the bottom of her toes as her medium length, thick, curly auburn hair tossed and swirled. She told stories so well that in a few years she was narrating on the radio for the La Crosse Children's Hour. Throughout her entire life, she loved to tell of my response one morning as I was one-stepping it down the deep blue carpeted stairway. "Karin, your toothbrush is dry," she called down to me from the bathroom. "Oops," I answered from my step, "I gess I dint buss my teef wiv da bussa—I buss em wiv da hanel." Mama Hon ran down the stairs and scooped me up, laughter-loving me till tears rolled down our faces. After we were out of cribs, her bedroom with Uncle Ernie was strictly off limits, seldom entered by Grandma or children. I felt privileged to sit at her dressing table and sniff her perfume only a few times during the years.

The grassy side yard that edged the walk and boulevard led to a more private garden in back where sky blue morning glories cascaded over a white trellis, and Mama Hon brushed my blond curls in the summer sunshine while Grandma tended her zinnias nearby, as taffy-colored Lady dog romped and chased the birds from their pedestal bath bordered by hydrangeas and daisies. Summer evenings often sparkled with lightning bugs that we tried to capture in mason jars.

Uncle Ernie was a mailman for most of the years I lived with my La Crosse family, and I still remember how special I felt at five when he took me along for part of his route. He also took me out on the Mississippi when he fished for bass or pike and threw back the strange looking catfish. He smoked a cigar and gave me the wrapper "rings." Warm weather signaled family adventures after church on Sunday. Monkey Island at the zoo was a favorite, and we'd stop for mugs of root beer on the way home. I remember picnics by Tadpole Pond across the long silver bridge, which was, at times, smothered by locusts in the summer, into

Minnesota; car rides around the Wisconsin countryside where we saw smoke rising from the teepees on the Indian reservations while we sang "Comin' 'Round the Mountain"; red barns and starched white farmhouses nestled in the rolling hills of dairy land, fields of golden corn nearby. We counted pure white horses shouting "Zoot!" only to have to "bury" them at the next cemetery and start all over again to see who got the most white horses. We took winding drives in the old green Plymouth up to Grand Dad's Bluff, which was propped by cushions of green hills, and we could see the whole town, the Mississippi and beyond. Life was simple, though unknown to us kids, financially very diffi-cult. This was still the Great Depression.

It was a treat to walk into town, past the "haunted house," and have my feet x-rayed at Bannisters before I could get a new pair of Mary Janes. Then we'd go have a soda and put a nickel in the jukebox. Sunday mornings, after

Grandma helped me dress and I admired her pearls, our family walked to the Congregational Church, where Uncle Ernie was a Trustee and I loved to sing "Onward Christian Soldiers."

I had a family in La Crosse, and I was their "Honey Girl," as Mama Hon called me. My mother visited me as often as she could, perhaps once a month. It was a four-hour train ride from Chicago. Though confused, I was generally happy to see her. I was just never sure what it meant when she appeared— would I stay or go with her? Who was this stylishly pretty woman who often arrived late at

20

night and peered in to see me, stay a day or two, and as soon as I got used to her face and voice, she'd leave again. The pattern of uncertainty began to grow in me. I had seen my father once as a three year old when he visited me in La Crosse. He and my mother eventually divorced and there was no further contact.

At the age of five, I began to travel from La Crosse to Chicago and back on the orange and black Hiawatha train, and I was in the care of a wonderfully caring and funny black porter by the name of George Washington. We sat together in the last seat so he could observe the passengers of the train car and we shared a sack lunch. We were happy, good friends and I loved wearing his red carnation on the lapel of my knitted navy and white sailor dress.

Life Gets Complicated

3

My mother remarried in Chicago, and she and Stan, who had proposed to her on the rooftop of the Palmolive Building, rented an apartment on the west side and sent for me to live with them. Because they both worked, a teenager named Dorothy was hired to take care of me during the summer. My older cousin, Ruthie, occasionally traveled from La Crosse to spend some time in the city and also to care for me. As fortunate as I was, when sick in bed one day, I felt so abandoned and distraught because my mother wasn't there that I opened the window and tearfully, shamefully thrust out my toys—including Honey Bear and my beloved Pooh books—one by one onto the pavement two stories below. When I entered first grade, I came home from school one day with such a large black eye from a gang bully that, seeing me coming, the janitor of our building took me into his basement apartment to show me, with boxing gloves, how to fight back and defend myself. I didn't want to fight, I wanted to play and be loved—I wanted my La Crosse Grandma's arms around me. Life was complicated in the big city.

My parents worked very hard and long hours, my mother now working in Stan's newly acquired exhibit and display business. She was also doing volunteer work for the Red Cross, and I was proud of her for doing that. I was seven when World War II began. To help the war effort, we peeled the tin foil off chewing gum wrappers and rolled it into balls that would be recycled for use in the defense plants. We had moved to another apartment building and on the corner was a Victory Garden. All who lived on that block shared in growing and eating the vegetables. My mother canned tomatoes at night and we felt fortunate to have enough tomato noodle casseroles to eat with crackers and milk for Sunday suppers. I was told about the starving children in Africa and frequently thought about them. I still agonize over the issue of waste and starvation. Since a child I've wondered, why not me? Why have I been *me* and not among the hungry and less fortunate in a far away, naked part of our world? We seldom attended church, but when we did, we drove in Stan's DeSoto with the musical horn to the Fourth Presbyterian Church on Michigan Avenue. I had been given a Bible by my Grandmother and loved looking at the pictures. I also kept close Lauren Ford's "The Little Book About God" that was given to me at age two.

Across the street lived a new friend, Mary Jane Hotter, who was a Catholic girl, and every time the bells rang from the large stone church on the other corner, we met in our hopscotch clothes and raced to a funeral, a wedding, a mass—for whatever occasion the bells were ringing. I sprinkled Holy Water from a little basin on the wall just inside and made the sign of the cross. I thought everyone in the world who wore a cross was Catholic—I wanted to belong and dutifully and respectfully knelt in the pews among the red flickering candles and statues of saints, learned the Rosary and thought I might become a nun.

I continued my railroad travels on the Hiawatha with my porter friend George Washington to spend many holidays in La Crosse. How I loved to pull into the outdoor station with giant cattails waving from the swamp along the track and to be scooped off the train amid laughter and joy. One time, my mother went with me, and from La Crosse we drove to her girlhood home in Galesville. She showed me the swinging bridge that she walked over to get to the one-room school house that had also been attended by her forever friend now in Peterborough, New Hampshire. She told me about her pony that the Indians had taught her to ride. They gave her the name of Princess Laughing Rain. We returned to La Crosse and the front porch where Grandma and Mama Hon were knitting argyle socks for the boys overseas, and Ruthie was dreaming about her soldier friend. Tired of small talk on a small front porch in a small town, my mother was anxious to leave.

She had become a city girl and had married a man who loved the city even more, especially Chicago. I always knew that my mother loved me—there was an unspoken bond between us, yet I yearned for the words of love. I also knew in my heart that she didn't know what to do with me. Because of my mother's inability to give of herself in a nurturing way, even though I was convinced of her love, I, nevertheless, wasn't sure just how important I was to her. I once scribbled and mailed her a note to the office that asked,

> I was your daughter yet Have you told the people that

I thought she might be ashamed of me and didn't want to tell her business associates that she had a daughter. Mama Hon was to tell me years later that my mother worshiped me like a Bible, but had to leave it sitting alone. She was not a natural mother. It wasn't easy for her. Motherhood didn't satisfy her quest for business excellence or fill her yearning to write plays or be on the stage. Her younger brother, Nick, had gone off to Hollywood, where he achieved fame and fortune as a film director. It was in their blood.

Scottish born Stan, whom I began to call Dad, focused his energies and talent almost exclusively on his business. I saw him Sunday mornings when he leisurely read the Chicago Tribune and late one or two evenings a week at the dinner table. "What did you do at school today, Karin?" I always knew his question was only to be polite, and after I said a few words, he returned to his favorite topic, which was his company. He never knew when I left the table. I hated those dinners and wondered why I was there. Didn't anyone want to share what was going on inside? I was not to complain—ever. The Depression was over and business improved, so it was possible for me to be taken out of the public school where the gangs had caused such fear in my mother that she insisted I be placed in a private school. I was a student at Francis W. Parker from second grade to the twelfth, and the school was to become like another family. At this four-story Tudor with wonderful nooks and crannies, wood floors, radiators and high ceilings, I enjoyed the art classes under roly poly Mrs. Clausinious. We painted and worked with clay. I still have the funny little figure I made of my mother wearing her Lily Dache hat. Field trips to the Chicago Art Museum motivated me early to experiment with sculpture, painting and charcoal drawing throughout my life. My mother presented me with a life membership in the institute that continues to remind me of her thoughtful generosity. Our class saw classic children's plays at Goodman Theater and heard beautiful music at Symphony Hall. May Day at FWP was my favorite time of year. Wearing peasant skirts and blouses, the girls, with pastel ribbons in hand, danced around the Maypole on the playing field. After the dance, when the design was intricately woven, a Scottish bagpiper led all of the children across the street to Lincoln Park where we had a picnic lunch and sang "Oh, The Days of the Kerry Dancers." I would then walk and dance and sing my way through the mile long park and climb the enormous seated statue of Thomas Jefferson, so I could sit high in his iron lap before going home.

We had moved to the third floor of a newer apartment building on the near north side across from Lincoln Park and a short distance from Lake Michigan. There was a long, grassy courtyard between our building and another—it was the opposite side where my forever friend Barbara lived with her widowed, working mother. Barbara and I, at age eight, played king and queen with oak leaves that we formed into crowns. We played jacks and hopscotch and sent secret messages to one another on a pulley we devised to go across the courtyard from her first floor window to mine on the third. My family had a back porch with a wooden railing that overlooked the alley and the roof of a small apartment hotel. And as I straddled the railing high above the concrete, I'd watch a young boy walk his pet duck with a leash on that flat roof and think it the funniest sight ever.

I began dancing lessons and took the city bus to the downtown Loop, where I learned ballet and tap in the little studio above a jewelry store. I loved reading the classics of *Heidi* and *Peter Pan*, Kate Seredy's beautifully illustrated *The Singing Tree* and *The Good Master*. I wept through *Beautiful Joe* and *Lassie*. I was given dolls that I loved—the Dionne

Patterns

Quints, Sonja Henie, Princess Elizabeth, and I played army nurse with lead soldiers and nurses and stretchers. I sent for Captain Midnight code watches and listened to The Lone Ranger. I cradled a baby doll with red curly hair and wished my mother would hold me. At Christmastime, she took me to Marshall Field's for lunch by the giant Christmas tree that was a few stories tall and decorated magically. And then I became aware of her drinking heavily and being out of control. Patterns of unpredictability were developing, and fear shook its ugly fist at us all.

*T*HE PATH OF PRETEND

4

*M*ama Hon began to call from La Crosse, and after hearing my mother's slurred voice, she frequently came to take me back to their home for a week or two where I was cuddled by Grandma. I felt secure in a family that was always there and never seemed to hurry, that laughed together and had laps to share and lived in a house that always looked the same.

Back in Chicago there were times that I was also taken by my dad to the suburban home of his parents. I adored my grandfather and spent hours sitting on the high stool in the basement watching as he stuffed the beautifully colored fragile pheasants he had hunted and brought home. Upstairs and away from his care was a different scene, and I became a bruised and frightened nine year old at the wicked hand of my paternal grandmother, and my overnight visits ended. I used to wonder if she was a witch.

I learned to live with fear and inconsistencies, yet the unique privileges that I experienced while growing up gave me a sense of anticipation and adventure as well as a lifelong appreciation for the arts. I began figure skating when nine years old, and how I loved the ice. I was a club member at the ice arena and felt exhilarated in a world of precisely disciplined school figures and exciting spins and jumps taught in private lessons by balding Bill Braun. I

learned to enjoy skating in some of the benefit programs that were organized for orphanages in the Chicago area, as well as in the Midwest senior ladies' competition later on. Dancing and skating were excellent physical outlets for me and they helped to develop skill and confidence. Going to my lessons was also far, far better than going home after school. Although she had her good times and could be fun to be with, all holidays were excuses for my mother to drink more, and she either loved me or hated me. I wondered if I was worth loving.

There was that Thanksgiving night in our apartment when I was awakened by crying and screaming that were louder than usual. I ran out into the hallway to see my dad striking my mother over and over again with his brown leather belt as she slumped to the floor against the wall. Hearing me begging him to stop, he turned to look at me and said, "Pretend you didn't see this, Karin." In my flannel nightie, I turned and ran out of the apartment, down the three flights of stairs and across the courtyard to the apartment of my friend Barbara and her mother. Mrs. K. cradled me in her arms until the sun rose.

Pretend seemed to be the answer for everything—where was *truth*? Why was truth hiding? My father became angry when my mother drank, but then he would drink as well. In my mind it was never a question of "What do I do about this?" or "Why is this happening?" Pretend. I had been told to pretend; therefore, I did not have to think about it. I must not listen to truth in our home. I must not tell. I must not feel. There was only one place where feelings were safe. They were safe inside of me.

It became more and more difficult for me to sleep, and little fears were following me like quiet shadows. I didn't know what might happen to my mother or to me, but I couldn't tell what I knew or felt to anyone. The summer after fourth grade, where I learned a lifetime history of Greece from the wonderful Miss Davis, I was told by my parents, "You need to go to California next week, Karin, and live with Aunt Alice." My role was not to complain and not to question. There was no discussion. A change was always "for the better." I needed to accept whatever that was and make the best of it. I didn't like leaving my friends, and what would happen at home while I was away? I was packed off for the summer and part of a school year to the lovely hills of suburban Flintridge.

I was back with the family that had first taken me in as an infant in Oshkosh and had subsequently moved to California. I secretly enjoyed the teasing of my uncle and boy cousins, and I watched in awe as Katherine dressed for her dates. We had a terrier dog named Penny, two riding horses and a sassy cow named Buttercup, who was supposed to stay in the corral that was fenced by my uncle. The joke was that he built it with the slats on the outside so that the cow had no trouble running right through the fence, especially when she was pregnant and in one of her moods. On one such day, I was taking Penny for a ride in the wagon down the driveway. Buttercup burst out of the corral suddenly and with such gusto that I grabbed the terrier and with her under my arm, climbed up the big, old oak tree. While the cow trampled the beautifully kept gardens and lawns of the neighbors, Penny and I sat near the top crook of the tree until my cousin Sumner came home from tennis and rescued us and the pregnant cow, now half a mile away. I loved being with my California family—the silliness and laughter—the quiet of the nights. The truth seemed "normal" here and there was usually someone at home because they wanted to be.

Because Uncle Nick was in the area directing his films, he visited and occasionally brought his Hollywood friends for a horseback ride through the upper hills and canyon and back for a big breakfast. I loved to sit in the kitchen with everyone around the table just talking and listening, as though their thoughts mattered. While Porter Jr. was figuring out how the telephone worked, Sumner took me on the back of the yellow motor scooter down the hill to the swimming pool. The family went faithfully to the LaCanada Presbyterian Church, where Aunt Alice was active in women's groups and Uncle Porter was an elder. I admired that and sensed a balance in their lives because of church involvement. Autumn arrived, and I easily adjusted to school there and loved the early walk down and over the hill with the sunshine gently sharing space with the morning fog. Tall trees shed their yellow green leaves as they formed an arbor for me. Beauty held my hand.

My mother wired shortly before Christmas to say that she missed me, and it was time for me to return to Chicago. I loved hearing her say that and hoped that I wouldn't have to pretend that home was normal this time. I renewed my commitment to figure skating and enjoyed catching the double decker bus where I could go up the winding stairway and sit on top with a view of Lake Michigan, the splendid old estates and apartment buildings with doormen who also walked the residents' dogs, women bundled up in fur coats, men racing for their blown-away hats. The bus made its way down Michigan Avenue; taxicabs honked and forced their way through traffic. Stunning shops, the famed Water Tower, the magnificent gray stone Fourth Presbyterian Church, office buildings and hotels were all reminders of the excitement of Chicago. Though not visible in the daylight, I knew the beacon from the Palmolive Building was sending out its illuminating beam like a circulating halo over the city and lake. Shortly before coming to the beautifully impressive Wrigley Building and Tribune Tower, I made my way down the narrow steps and got off at the next bus stop. With the new skating outfit Grandma Lena had made, I hurried briskly against the wind for the few blocks to the ice arena.

I had met another friend through skating, and we sometimes went to her home afterward, although we much preferred window shopping. Her mother also drank heavily, and the last time I was in their apartment, we heard loud noises from down the hall. Looking toward the kitchen, we saw her drunken mother being sexually assaulted on the table. At least *that* never happened at my house, and I looked the other way and told no one. Those kinds of things had to be forgotten. Yet I never forgot.

I seldom went home after school. There was usually no one there unless my mother had decided to come home early from the office. And I didn't want to know about it. The only reason she was ever home sooner than six o'clock was because she *needed* to begin drinking earlier. She didn't like me to be in the kitchen because I'd look for bottles of liquor to throw out. I felt extremely isolated in my thoughts and my circumstances and I was fearful being alone. So I took the bus or streetcar to the homes of my friends— Wendy, who used to tell me that I was too young to have worry lines on my forehead and had a Dachshund named Noodle, and Hawley owned an Orphan Annie dog that was blind. The Moms of Sue and Linda and Nancy were always home. I felt safe and non-threatened in those environments. My forever friend Barbara began to attend FWP, and we walked to school together or took the bus in bad weather. She had attended a Chicago boarding school earlier and also loved the beacon that, as a lonely child, she could watch from her bedroom window while it cast its stream of light through the sky like a sentinel for her. When we walked through Lincoln Park, we toured the humid conservatory on our way and loved the hundreds of tulips that bloomed alongside in the spring. At the end of the day, we'd check on the elephants in the zoo at the other end of the park, throw an ice cream cone through the grilled cage to our favorite brown and cream bear that stood on his hind legs to catch his treat, and we'd run for our lives from the slimy snakes even though in their cages. Sometimes on a Wednesday afternoon, we'd walk over to Clark Street to see Barbara's mother at the Christian Science Reading Room where she stopped after work, then 'round the corner to the bakery for chocolate eclairs or the Jewish deli for huge pickles and sausage. Saturdays were spent with my friends at the movies—Tarzan and Jane, musicals and ice-skating extravaganzas with Sonja Henie. We cried through My Friend Flicka and Bambi. On occasion my mother took me shopping on a Saturday, and we went over the bridge to the Loop or we poked around the shops on Michigan Avenue. We were amused by the silly monkey wearing a purple pill box hat and red satin skirt while dancing to the organ grinder's tune as we tossed pennies on the corner of Michigan and Oak. I loved spending time with my mother that was real—times I could talk about and didn't have to pretend. She appeared normal, and it felt good to be her daughter.

After my Chicago grandfather died, we visited the cemetery every Sunday afternoon. Gladiolus became my least favorite flower, the grave flower. On Sunday evenings I walked down the street with Barbara and her mother to the large, round, white Christian Science Temple that took over the whole next block. It was a fascinating place to me, and I looked forward to going there even though I was somewhat confused by the people who stood up to share their physical healings.

My St. Patrick's Day birthdays were celebrated at school every year, where, at noon in the cafeteria, a bouquet of green carnations and a beautifully decorated store-bought cake were delivered for me, from my mother, to share with my classmates. It made me feel uncomfortable and special at the same time. The secret within was that I longed for my mother to bake me a cake. Just once. Now that would be special!

The year that I was twelve and in the seventh grade, Stan, who had been acting the role of father for several years, now decided to legally adopt me. I always thought my mother had probably talked him into it. After the courthouse procedure that morning, I handed a note to my teacher that explained why I was late to school. Miss Greenebaum looked up at me from behind her desk, her magnified albino eyes behind thick glasses framed by her bobbed green-blond hair, and said how wonderful that I had been adopted. She congratulated me. I was not only surprised at her reaction of delight, but I was confused. My mind saw it all so differently—what was wrong with me that he had waited so long?

There were a couple of summers that I went with my parents to Basswood Lodge north of Ely, Minnesota, and I swam in the lake, went fishing, was "held up" in the outhouse (before the lodge installed cabin plumbing) by a black bear, and I learned to love blueberries. My mother didn't drink very much on those vacations, so our mealtimes in the lodge were fun and without embarrassment. I also spent summers in La Crosse and went to summer camp with Barbara, where we learned to paddle a canoe and sing camp songs around the bonfire as the loons flew over the peaceful waters in the dark of the woods under Wisconsin skies.

*T*HE BROWNSTONE

5

*W*e moved yet again to a charming old red-brick brownstone with black shutters and an iron gate. My mother remodeled the home extensively and furnished it with treasures found at estate sales. A marble topped chest from the Potter Palmer mansion, oriental rugs and a beige velvet sofa graced the living room, where she had the walls between two parlors removed to open up a stunning room with coral shutters on the tall front windows. And it was in that plaid chair by the window where I hated to see her— the mother who was fashionable and fun, much loved by her family and friends, who enjoyed entertaining, was a fair and honest person, thought by many to be brilliant. Tasteful, she had an eye for decorating and for dressing in the latest Vogue styles. She was known for her collection of hats. She had her dream house and the ability to furnish it according to her fancy. Her heart was tender and her life *should* have been one of beauty and joy. Who would believe that she lived a life of deep pain and anguish because of the vicious betrayal of alcoholism. When she was under the influence of liquor, a corner of the living room became a scene of tragedy. Her composure was lost. Her stately presence was slumped in that plaid chair, legs bowed in front of her with one arm down the side clutching the whiskey bottle, the other loosely holding onto her cigarette that was dropping long ashes into the blue Venetian glass ashtray on the floor below. On her face was the look that said it all—helplessness and shame, fear and repulsion, inner friction and a defiant spirit. She was unable to focus her eyes and they rolled as if lost in a realm of nothingness, and her tongue spoke harsh words that denied her real goodness and dishonored her heart.

I hated the pattern of pretend—I saw what was true when I came home from school, but it was becoming so frequent that I didn't know what to do but to pretend and freeze my feelings of painful disappointment. She called out to me, "Karin, you are so pretty—you are everything to me—Karin, you are a slut—you'll never make it in this world—Karin, don't leave me." I walked past her into the kitchen to make a sandwich or a bowl of cereal for my dinner to take up the curved mahogany staircase to my room down the hall. She continued to cry and to curse in lonely confusion. I knew she didn't want to be like that—who on earth would choose to be an alcoholic? Who would willingly let alcohol take the controls? No one in their right mind! I locked my bedroom door away from the repugnant air and the figure that was lost in it. The late night hours were sure to be noisy. I did my homework. Then, as I tried to sleep, burying my head under the covers, I heard her making her way up the stairs. She fell onto the carpeted hallway where she would crawl and stand and fall again amidst her crying out my name and that of "Stanley." She got sick on the bathroom floor and crawled back to the hallway where she lay weak and tormented—an agony of the mind and spirit and flesh. And I swore to myself I'd never be like her.

My father was often out of town during the worst episodes, or he worked late and stopped for dinner on the way home, where he would then have a couple of martinis while catching up with the news on the radio before going to bed. On occasion, he stayed in a nearby hotel for the night.

I could never get over how strong my mother was when she was drinking. The physical strength in her arms was something to be reckoned with late one night. In a rage, because I had emptied her purse so she couldn't buy more liquor, she pounded on my bedroom door and screamed that she had to see me. When I unlocked the door, her figure was unsteady, arms flailing about and in one hand a large butcher knife. Her face appeared gray and her eyes rolled in mocking anger, while I quickly slid into my closet, trying to close the double doors. She held onto my wrist with such force that marks from that "vice" were left for several hours. I was frightened and confused as to how to handle this woman, my own mother—was this the end or just another nightmare? I loved her. I hated what she turned into when she drank. It wasn't the real person, and I knew that in my heart. Love fought hate in order to survive. We wrestled in my closet, the knife dangerously close at times to each of us. She eventually weakened and abruptly left the room, holding the knife and crying out for forgiveness, and much later in the night, I covered her with a warm blanket as she lay sleeping on the hallway floor outside my room.

*M*OODS OF CHANGE

6

*D*uring my thirteenth summer, when I was visiting my California family, my Mother and Dad decided to fly out. Grandma and Mama Hon and Uncle Ernie were coming as well. Their La Crosse minister from the Congregational Church was going to be in the L.A. area and it seemed a good idea for everyone to gather at the Malibu Beach home of my Uncle Nick and his current movie actress wife and their two children, so that there could be a baptism. With a sweeping view of the magnificent Pacific Ocean, its diamond white waves splashing and foaming onto the warm sandy shore, the sunny patio was protected from the salty breezes. Surrounded by family and an abundance of potted tangerine geraniums, my father, my new little cousin Timmy—Nick and Gloria's son—and I were baptized. I don't recall the words or the reasons expressed. I vividly remember the value of being together in a joyfully relaxed mood that was unfamiliar to me when my parents were present.

Back together in Chicago, we did a few things other than cemetery trips on Sundays. We went to The Palmer

House or the Drake Hotel for dinner, which was lovely, although it began with my parents' cocktails, which was invariably a forewarning of what the night at home would be. We listened to and laughed at Jack Benny on the radio, and we sat on the back porch and read the funnies while Dad rolled and chewed his LaPalina from one side of his mouth to the other, and we went to his office, where I was fascinated by the three-dimensional trade show and museum exhibits being designed and built in the plant. My father was an excellent businessman and fine communicator in that world, but he did not have the ability or the desire to speak and listen to young people. It was inevitable that he would laugh at me when I tried very hard to convey a serious thought. I was unable to say anything to him that was heard. It made me feel like a burden rather than an individual. He did not want to listen to any concerns about my mother—"She'll be fine," he'd say, and that was that. My mother lived with fears that she might lose me and was terrified when I was sick in bed. Unless it was unavoidable, I just didn't tell anyone when I wasn't feeling well. Home was where my family was—but without honesty and predictability—with the nonverbal agreement that we did not tell, did not feel, did not trust. Home was not a safe place to be, and I would have a home someday that would never, ever be like that.

I continued my figure skating and ballet, and my mother decided I should attend Fort Nightly, an etiquette and ballroom dance class for girls and boys that was held once a week in a private club. We wore dresses, coats and ties, white gloves and we were trained in manners, proper curtsy and dance, including the waltz. There were times I felt very spoiled in addition to knowing I was most fortunate to have so many cultural advantages. I tried to contribute some joy to my parents over the years.

On the first day of eighth grade, my forever friend Barbara and I looked up from our desks to stare at a new boy as he walked into our classroom. He was tall, broad-shouldered and he resembled the movie star, Van Johnson, our heartthrob. His name was Bill, and I experienced my first crush. Groups of us went on the streetcar to O'Connell's on Saturdays for hamburgers before an Esther Williams movie or romantic war picture. Our entire class was annually invited to Nancy's summer home in the Indiana Dunes for a weekend. We took the old Illinois Central train and held our noses as we traveled near the soap factories and through the steel mills of Gary, Indiana.

Halfway through my freshman year at FWP, Dad admitted my mother to a sanitarium for a week of "recovery." It was the only time he ever took a serious step toward her physical well-being. I was sent off to California again, and though I hated to leave my school friends, I was accustomed to change and happy for a warm retreat. Easter in Flintridge was wonderful. After church, it seemed like a hundred eggs had been hidden among the daylilies and roses near the saucer magnolia. We hunted until our baskets were

full, then gathered around the dining room table for a meal of creamed chicken in noodle nests. Friends as well as family celebrated the risen Christ, whatever that meant.

The patio was a favorite place for the family to visit or to sit alone under the pineapple palm—quiet, private and happy. I also loved to sit under the arbor of pink climbing Cecil Bruner sweetheart

43

roses nearby. Night sounds in Flintridge came from the Dodgers baseball games Aunt Alice listened to on the radio and from the police reports that Uncle Porter tuned into on his short-wave. My cousin Sumner took me out in his Ford coup with his friends and tried to teach me how to drive in the foothills.

I returned to Chicago in June to look for a job and found one at the Carson Pirie & Scott department store in the city. It was a modeling position for the advertising department that was on the top floor sharing space with inventory storage. Although fans circulated, it was especially hot for those of us modeling because we had to dress in winter clothing and pose for as long a time as the illustrators needed while they drew the ads for the upcoming seasons in the newspapers. Yet I enjoyed the job, the fashion and the discount benefits, and worked there again the following summer. My mother fell back into the same old pattern. It was fairly obvious to me that when she was drinking and in that weakened state of mind, an evil force overtook her and she became something she was not. I remembered Aunt Alice telling me how she and her sister were the ones to retrieve their drunken father, my maternal grandfather, time after time from the Galesville jail where he was thrown after wild sprees. The year would come when their beloved younger brother, my uncle, would die of a brain tumor, alone and penniless all because of alcoholism. Other family members would succumb to this hateful disease of the mind and body. The pattern seemed to have been established in their chemistry make-up long ago. So little known, nothing to discuss, a private shame.

The Old School

courtesy of Francis W. Parker

*C*IFE SAVERS

7

*A*fter skating in the ladies' Midwest championship competition, I reluctantly gave it up. The schedule was too demanding, and I was unprepared to handle it all. I gave up ballet as well but remained very involved with after-school sports. I loved playing left wing for our field hockey team and didn't get home until dark. I didn't pursue a leadership role at FWP and never attempted to get very good grades—adequate would be fine. It was important to me that I not do anything to draw attention, that I just stay busy and look okay so I wouldn't stand out and be noticed. I wanted to be average and even changed the spelling of my name to be the same as the one other Karen in our school.

I seldom took time to analyze my thoughts or home situation. What happened just plain happened, and I was expected to react accordingly. I did feel different and it was hard to get enough sleep, so I'd place ice bags under my eyes many mornings to remove the puffiness. I truly didn't care *if* I didn't sleep; I just couldn't let it show—that could reveal a problem that had to be hidden. It was becoming difficult to concentrate on a heavier load of homework, and I was scared to death of severe Miss Cornell, with her tightly pulled back white hair bun, in social studies, where she made me sit in the front row. There were a few times after school that I spent in the principal's office making up my homework. Mr. Smith was to tell me years later at an FWP reunion that he, as principal, always did worry about me and knew something about the problem at home. Even then, I didn't offer a word of further explanation. I continued to protect my secret. Strange that I could be so loyal when, by most people's standards, it was undeserved. I felt that it was a huge risk to expose my mother's misunderstood illness. Humiliation, rejection, judgment—all of which I presumed would be the result of disclosure. I recognized and was grateful for the unconditional friendship and protection given me by my classmates and most of the faculty. At their kind invitation, I occasionally went to the home of Peggy, my gym teacher or to the Ellisons', English teachers, where I could study at night and no questions were asked.

FWP was a family unit in my life. My mother couldn't have made a better decision than when she placed me in that school at age seven. I loved our Big and Little Sister program and still remember the older sister of one of my classmates taking me by the hand. I would follow suit later when I led little Ann around. We wore uniforms in high school, and I thought I'd never again look at a navy skirt. Some of the students were on full scholarships, and the majority of the students from kindergarten through twelfth grade were Jewish—many from prominent Chicago families. Some arrived at school in the morning in sleek black Cadillacs driven by their family chauffeur. We all worked together in the annual toy shop to make toys for the underprivileged children in the inner city at Christmastime. We sang Handel's Messiah under the leadership of "Griff" every year that I can remember. And most of us began to date. We went to sock hops and the movies, football and basketball games, to proms with gardenia corsages and danced to "In the Still of the Night." We dated boys from other private schools and I sometimes went out with Bill. I usually spent the night at Barbara's to avoid a date being confronted by my mother or having to hear the fighting screams from both my parents from outside the front door.

Love walked into my life during high school. Chris— tall and slender, khakis and light blue shirt with cuffs rolled, handsome and intelligent, news editor and baseball player, gentle and fun—became my closest friend. We rode in his little yellow Crosley and sometimes got stopped by the snow drifts. We attended Christmas Eve services at the cathedral off Michigan Avenue though he was part Jewish. In his wonderful deep voice he read the Song of Songs to me from the Bible, and we read together "The Prophet" and Walt Whitman's "Leaves of Grass." He bought me nosegays of purple violets from the corner flower vendor on Rush Street, and we walked hand in hand as we laughed and shared our innermost thoughts. We sat under the stars listening to the extraordinarily beautiful classical music at Ravinia, and danced to "You'll Never Walk Alone" and "Honey." There was "no end to our tomorrows."

PATTERNS OF THE HEART

8

A battlefield was raging at home, and by now, my grades were slipping, so my mother decided I should go to Wayland Academy, a private coed high school in Wisconsin, for my senior year. I hated the idea of leaving even though I had to believe it was for the best. Chris was a year ahead of me and was preparing for college in Oregon. He sweetly helped me to adjust to the decision. It turned out to be a good year, a positive experience and my first with dorm living. I made more lifelong friends, and early morning chapel was a requirement that I loved. Most of us attended the Baptist church in town on Sundays, where the preacher was also the deeply respected Wayland coach. I still remember having a serious kidney infection that year and, from my window in the Catholic hospital, watching in amazement as the nuns in their black habits played softball on the field. My grades greatly improved, we popped popcorn on the radiator in our room, and I was dating a handsome track star. Chris and I had agreed to date others that year but could hardly wait for summer. My mother thought he was terrific and had given him one of his summer jobs of mowing our lawn.

I really wanted to go to Mills College in California, but reluctantly agreed to enroll in a small private college in southern Illinois to satisfy my mother who now wanted me closer to home. My major was art, and because of a fabulous instructor at Monticello, I did well. I exhibited some work at the St. Louis Art Museum and generally enjoyed my life on campus—it was a beautiful and peaceful one, but I missed my love in the Pacific Northwest. I was casually dating one of the town boys from Alton, and I periodically saw Bill when he invited me up to the University of Illinois football games and the Alpha Chi Rho fraternity parties.

The following spring, Chris asked if I'd like to spend the break on the campus of his school. I couldn't get over the beauty of Oregon. Mt. Hood was a breathtaking sight as we drove up the mountain road, walls of snow on either side, to reach Timberline Lodge on a clear cold day. Back in Portland we went out for a pizza dinner with a group of his college friends including one of the girls from the dorm where I was staying—and something was wrong. She was engaged to someone else, but there was a startling exchange of glances between them. What was happening? I was very frightened, and our relationship was not the same when I left at the end of the week.

It was May at Monticello. Though I was deeply hurting on the inside, it seemed like the whole world was in bloom. Several of us liked to go hiking and spelunking among the river caves. After climbing up the hill following one of our adventures, the town boy I had casually dated during the year suddenly pulled me behind a tree and proposed. Larry was handsome with dark wavy hair and he stood six feet four. He told me how I was unlike any other girl he had known because I would go no further than kissing. He respected and loved me and wanted me for his wife. I didn't think about being vulnerable or about being rational and planning for the future. Both Chris and I had been hurt and it would soon be time for me to think about returning to Chicago for the summer, the very last place I wanted to be. It was a good feeling to be wanted by this nice and decent guy who was also lots of fun, and I thought I could love him—at least I could pretend. Larry and I eloped the following weekend. We were married in the dark of night by a justice of the peace somewhere in southern Illinois. This could be a new beginning, and I had an opportunity to make someone happy and to establish our own home.

I later suspected my roommate of communicating my sudden plans to my parents. Upon hearing of our elopement after trying in vain to stop it by contacting the police—who looked for our car—unknown to me, my father reached me by phone to ask, "Karen, did you *have* to get married?" His words stung to my very core—it didn't occur to me that he or anyone might consider that purity and intimacy before marriage were not important to me. My values had always been old fashioned, my moral standards high with no room for compromise. What hurt me the most was that my father really didn't know me very well, and he placed an unfounded judgment on me. It was during a discussion on values that a longtime friend was to ask me years later, "Karen, where did you get your sense of goodness?" It was simply a part of me.

My mother wanted to give us a wedding reception in the garden of their brownstone. She knew how to entertain and had a green thumb that she used to make the side yard quite charming with well-designed private areas featuring specimen trees and sensational geraniums. After the lovely event, Larry and I returned to our apartment in Alton where he worked hard in the grocery store and I looked for a job. I became pregnant and though we were ecstatic about the baby, I was ill with morning sickness that wouldn't quit. I was also lonely. I missed my friends—my own friends. I missed the big city. Larry was still a small town boy. Like my mother, I had become a city girl. The theater, music, art, excitement were all far away. I felt very isolated, and I was. Our marriage was becoming shallow as we faced the reality that we had never had anything in common. We didn't know how to compromise. This wasn't supposed to happen, but finally truth was more important than pretend, and late that summer after only a few months of married life, we separated. Having nowhere else to go and without any money, I was forced to return to my parents' house and back into my pink and white bedroom up the stairs and down the hall. It seemed like a nightmare I was used to but had tried to run away from. I took long walks and plenty of iron supplements to build myself up from an anemic condition. I didn't have control of my life yet was grateful for a warm place to live and food to eat.

When on the stand in the divorce court, the judge looked at me in astonishment. "Is thirty-five dollars a month really adequate?" he asked. The attorney for my parents responded positively. They were financially able to care for me and the baby, and because of my poor health, I needed rest. Though feeling manipulated, all I could do on the stand was nod my head in agreement and the decree was awarded. I was not to see Larry again, nor did he ever make an attempt to see our child. As we were to learn years later, he died prematurely of a heart attack.

There was a day when Chris appeared at the house to pick up the books he had loaned me and the ones we read together in years past—when we were friends and in love. With misunderstanding, tears and bitterness, we had few words for one another and we parted company. The following year he married the girl who stole his glances.

THE LIGHT OF THE BEACON

9

The months were shockingly lonely. My friends were away at college. Chicago appeared dark and naked, its charcoal winter trees dead, a fleece blanket of snow blew around the edges and sometimes lifted to reveal the soot of the city. Waves from Lake Michigan smacked against the seawall and the spray froze in midair to look like frost-bearded gnomes guarding the cold sand beach.

But that splendid beacon on top of the Palmolive Building—a fixture for many years that served as a guide for aircraft—continued its nightly circular vigil around the city. I loved the beacon as my mother had loved it when she was a young woman alone in Chicago. It was a light and a constant. It filled a need.

One day I drove my mother's car out into the country and found Orphans of the Storm, a kennel that housed animals for adoption. There was the dog I was to name Chrissy, a beautiful black and white Welsh springer spaniel with thick wavy fur and paws, a blaze of white on her forehead. I took her home where at night she lay on the rug beside my bed, and with her sweet brown eyes of love, Chrissy would look up at me and we'd "talk." I knew I could trust her to never tell of my tears. She was to be a loyal member of my family for fourteen more years.

There was finally a reason to like February in Chicago. My beautiful fair-haired daughter was born. She was the real goodness that came out of my marriage. While I was in the hospital, my mother thoughtfully fixed up an apartment in the basement for us, and Julie, Chrissy and I had a place of our own, even though we were financially governed from upstairs. Unpredictability was a daily consequence of alcoholism, and it was my mother who held the purse strings and who made the decisions regarding Julie's pediatric care. Because of her inconsistencies, I took my baby to the best pediatrician in the city or stood in line with the other young moms at the welfare clinic. There was no conventional conformity, and I had no freedom to plan. I could only guess at what my mother's determinations might be.

I took Julie and Chrissy for long walks through Lincoln Park by the statue I used to climb and around the lagoon where old men were feeding the ducks and young couples were smiling at one another as their row boats drifted. We smelled the tulips by the humid conservatory. The bear that loved ice cream was still there. We spread a blanket on the grass where I had picnicked with my classmates which didn't seem to be too many years earlier. Strolling back to the brownstone, I was relieved that we had an outside entrance to our basement apartment and a hot plate in the kitchen area so we could eat our meals without friction and without exposure to the deteriorating situation on the floors above. I could frequently hear the sounds of crying and screaming, doors slamming, and I knew from the past how to picture the drunken scene that I had tried to escape. I loved being a mom, and I was going to be a good mom, so help me.

TURNING POINTS

10

My friend Bill, whom I had first met in eighth grade at FWP and had dated off and on, resurfaced and we began to date. He loved Julie and our dog, and he and I fell in love. A tall and handsome football player, strong and stable, consistent and reliable—unconditional love for me—too good to be true. His family was active in the Ravenswood Presbyterian Church, and the following September, Bill and I were married in the chapel there. The day began with storm clouds and intermittent rain. As Dr. Wright, who had married my parents a few years earlier in the Fourth Presbyterian Church, pronounced us man and wife, we turned to see the sun streaming in through the exquisite stained glass windows and a glorious rainbow appeared when we stepped outside the chapel doors.

We had a one night honeymoon at the Edgewater Beach Hotel, a sprawling pink landmark that sat on the edge of Lake Michigan. One dozen beautiful deep-red, long-stem roses graced the wide entry to our hotel room—a surprise from Len, another forever friend since fifth grade and Bill's best man. Bill and I danced to the live big band sounds of Tommy Dorsey on the Promenade by the moonlight over the water.

We purchased our first home in Northbrook—a forty minute drive from Chicago, and our lives were happy. There was no pretend. Bill legally adopted Julie one year after our wedding and two years later our adorable saucer-eyed brunette, Barbara Anne, whose pediatrician called her the Campbell Soup Baby, was born. Bill and I spent the evenings folding diapers as we caught up with each other's day. We played bridge with the neighbors on weekends and occasionally put the children on mattresses in the back of our station wagon and went to the drive-in theater.

My next pregnancy lasted almost seven months. After two days of hospitalization at Wesley Memorial, my placenta ruptured, and I had an emergency cesarean section. Our first little boy, "perfect in form," weighed one and a half pounds and lived for a night and day. We never saw him or held him. Never said hello or good-bye. We signed papers to release little Peter John to research, and I left the hospital with empty arms and a memory held so close only a heart can see.

Grandma Lena died in La Crosse, and I couldn't attend the funeral. As soon as I was strong enough, Bill and I took our little girls to see the bluffs and the Mississippi and we spent time with Mama Hon and Uncle Ernie in their new home in the hills overlooking the valley. As I listened to my uncle telling about his membership with the Masonic Lodge, I recalled the choices made by my mother's and Mama Hon's father years before in Galesville, and why the family changed from the Lutheran to the Congregational church.

Visits to the Chicago home of my parents were infrequent, and new members of my family couldn't understand why I wouldn't take the children there for most Christmases and holidays. They didn't understand that I couldn't trust the behavior of my mother. She may have seemed fine over the phone to them in the morning, but I knew how hard it was to predict what evening might bring. I not only wanted to protect my little girls—I wanted to protect the image of their Grandmother. The solution was for us to keep our home open to my parents, and though we had liquor in the house, my mother wouldn't have access to it. There were times when my father called to cancel their arrival because heavy drinking had taken hold. Thus, I was able to have some control over our family gatherings.

My father continued to travel a great deal, and one time when he was in New York, my mother called. It was late at night, and she begged that I drive into the city and take her to the hospital. When I saw her staggered anguish, the lostness of her eyes and fragility of her bruised body from falling in her home, I called her doctor who made arrangements for her to be admitted to the psychiatric ward at Wesley Memorial Hospital. It was not a struggle to take her. She was weak and frail and crying, but she let me support and guide her. The nurse took us through the double

locked doors to a small, spare, gray room with a single bed and bars on the window. I stood before my mother as she sat high on the bed, thin black and blue legs dangling over the side, white hospital gown and tears streaming down her face. Fear in those eyes. Fear of what might happen, or might not happen, if left in this place. "Help me. Don't leave me. I need help. Please." Her sorrow, and mine, tore passionately through my very being as I turned and walked away—unable to look back. Alcoholism was like a plague that dominated her soul and robbed her body and mind of all that was good and reasonable. She wanted to be free of that curse. She needed to be left in order to begin getting well at the hands of medical experts. The nurse unlocked the unit doors, and I hurried onto the elevator. I'd see her tomorrow and be able to comfort her. I drove home trying to maintain my composure, reassuring myself that my mother was safe—that this was a chance for a new beginning. A new pattern. One of truth that could be not only tolerated and accepted, it could be victorious.

When my father returned a few days later he was annoyed at her hospitalization and said he needed her at the office. When he visited her he thought she was doing "just fine" and he made the decision to release her. Hopelessness replaced the hope. The opportunity for competent medical help had been taken away—stolen. It was selfish, and it was difficult for me to ever forgive him. It was as though my mother had lost her future. There was no new pattern.

*B*EAUTY BEGETS BROKENNESS

11

*I*n 1961, Bill and I, our children and Chrissy dog moved to southern California, where we bought a charming small brick home in LaCanada. It was good to see the mountains again that had always symbolized strength for me. The Sierra Madre foothills were directly behind and above us. I loved being in beautiful country with orange and lemon trees in my own back yard, and it was wonderful to be close to the Flintridge home of Aunt Alice and family.

On the steps below the used brick patio one Saturday morning, I invited Julie to sit with me while I told the story of her adoption by Bill. With her blond hair gently glistening in the sunlight, pale blue liquid eyes highlighted by long black lashes, arms folded around her knees, she listened intently. When finished, I asked, "Any questions, Julie?" She gave me a hug and asked where her daddy was. Bill was working in the garage and she ran to him. Looking up at this gentle man she adored, she asked if he would sterilize a pin, then prick each of their fingers and rub them together. They would "then be blood relatives."

Our son, David, was born the following year at Huntington Memorial Hospital in Pasadena. This C-section was different, and as my doctor held him up in front of me while he cut the umbilical cord, I wept with joy as I saw this perfect little blond healthy boy. Our family was complete. The girls had been christened as babies back in Chicago. David's christening took place at LaCanada's Presbyterian Church where I had gone as a school girl with my California family.

Less than a year later, after my parents' travels to Russia and one week before they were to visit us and see their only grandson for the first time, my father called me from New York where he had gone on business. It was his birthday, in February, and he had just received news of my mother's death. She had died in a fire in their Chicago brownstone. I listened quietly as he spoke. So quiet that at one point he asked, "Are you there, Karen?" I was numb. The single thought that interrupted me was, "I knew it." I expressed to my dad how sorry I was and told him we'd be there the next day. When I called my cousin, now living in Pennsylvania, her first response was, "I knew it." Because of my mother's drinking and smoking and being left alone so often, Gretchen and I had long ago shared the fear that she might die in a fire. Yet the reality burned like a shock wave through me, and I was never to be the same.

The fire had started in my old room that she had turned into a study. She had been drinking and had fallen asleep with a cigarette in her hand. It began to burn into the upholstery of the small sofa where she was sitting. Awakened by the smoke, she tried to make her way down the hall to escape. My mother was found on the upstairs landing after firemen made an opening through the roof to release the dense billows of smoke. She suffered burns on her back and hands—her death was by asphyxiation. When Bill and

I arrived at the funeral parlor and saw her in the casket, I knew she must be somewhere else—that this was really not the end. I wept inside not only for the terrible loss I felt, the tragedy of her life and her death at sixty years old, but because of her magical beauty. Her face was never so peaceful; it was without fear or pain, without a flaw. She looked free, and I could hardly take my eyes off of her.

Mama Hon had gotten there first and selected a lovely pale blue dress with long sleeves that could be pulled over my mother's burned hands. Her service was held in the funeral home's chapel and it looked like an English garden in full bloom. All who knew and loved her were aware of her touch for beauty and romance with flowers.

The following two weeks were bleak in Chicago's cold gray days of winter when even the trees looked like death. Bill had returned to California, and I stayed in a hotel with my dad nearby. He was devastated, but I didn't know how to talk to him. We had never shared a conversation. The house needed to be inventoried and insurance claims filed. He left me in charge.

Each day was like crawling through a lifeless, cold swamp of black soot. Lingering smokiness filled my nostrils in a house that held few good memories. Yet it was her house, not mine, and she had loved it dearly. I felt driven to search for each book, vase, photograph, pearl, anything that had belonged to her. The plays she had written were destroyed. Most family photograph albums and scrapbooks gone. Many pieces of their beautiful antique furniture and virtually all their clothing was irretrievably smoke or water damaged. I was groping beyond the shock of the atrocity for something physical to hold on to—something good, worthwhile and true. Feelings could wait.

On a lonely trip home to southern California, I was seated next to a window on the plane, looking out at the clear blue sky. Suddenly there appeared a very distinctive oval picture frame. Inside the translucent white oval was the life-size head and pale blue-gowned shoulders of my mother. There was a sweet smile on her face. At that moment, as I fixed my gaze upon her, I knew in my heart that she was in heaven. It was an unexplainable gift and one that I could hold on to forever.

Physically far away from the harshness of her winter death in Chicago, but unable to understand or to focus on the gift I had been given, I began to experience nightmares. Scenes of the fire flashed in my mind, and I awakened in fearful tears. To help me get back to sleep, Bill would make me a hot toddy. As the weeks and months of sleepless nights went by, I'd often sneak in a second hot toddy and maybe even a third. They helped me sleep and occasionally freed me of the nightmares.

Bill and I had had drinks before—with neighbors—out to dinner—nothing unusual had ever happened. We had liquor in the house and hadn't thought twice about it—not only that, but it would never happen to me. I had loved my mother, but I had spent years swearing I'd never be like her. Unaware that I was suppressing my feelings, I was *fine* as always. After all, I was strong and I had control. I protected my mother's death as I had tried to protect her life. I explained to anyone who asked that she died in an electrical fire. I pretended. The truth was too painful. And I *needed* something to help cope with the pain. A hot toddy certainly wasn't interfering with my ability to function the next day. In fact, because it enabled me to sleep, it helped. Sedated sorrow . . .

We joined the mariners group in our church and had good friends and neighbors. Our children were happy and healthy, and Bill enjoyed his job in the trade show industry. However, my father requested that we move back to Chicago so that Bill could help him in his business there. He wanted family nearby. He missed his grandchildren.

Our family, dog and all, boarded the train for Illinois. We stopped to say hello to wonderful San Francisco where Chrissy dog stayed with us at the elite St. Francis for a few days. We then continued our adventure through the Feather River Canyon winding our way and our hearts out of the beauty of mountains and valleys, to travel the flatlands of the Midwest and arrive at Chicago's Union Station.

SUPERMOM—PERFECT HOME
12

We moved into a lovely five-bedroom Colonial home in Northbrook with a rose garden off the enclosed porch. Though careful, we had no financial worries. Bill thrived in the exhibit and display business and worked long days into nights. He did some traveling and we visited interesting and exotic places for national conventions, and we drank and smoked like the rest of the people. Together and separately, we worked hard and we played hard. We had good friends, and our social calendar was full. I played tennis, and Bill played golf with his forever friend Len who had settled in Northbrook with his wife. I was the super-responsible "supermom." A driving desire was within me to be the perfect wife and the perfect mother, and I could see no reason why I couldn't be the perfect community participant as well. I yearned to provide the atmosphere in our home that would be safe and honest, kind and accepting, harmonious, fun and nonjudgmental, loving. I would be guessing at what was "normal" for the next twenty years.

I read to my children—*The Little Book about God, Winnie the Pooh, Heidi*—and I took them to Ravinia on Saturdays where they saw Leonard Bernstein conduct Peter and the Wolf. I made some of the girls' clothing and nursed them all back to health—Barbie Anne and David suffered from chronic bronchitis and asthma. I baked the birthday cakes and made cookies, drove the girls to their dancing lessons, ice skating and to choir practice at the Village Church. They were in Brownies and Girl Scouts and had slumber parties. I took them to the Art Institute and every museum in the city, and we all loved every minute.

Our beloved Chrissy dog had to be put to sleep after her whole system let down from old age. Her eyes of love and loyalty held our emotions gently as Barbie and I said good-bye in the veterinarian's waiting room. Chrissy had even let our children dress her for Halloween, including a funny mask and jewelry; had slept under the crib of each one and protected them like an old-fashioned nanny; and had been my confidante and pal for fourteen years. One of a kind—and I'd miss her.

I was on the PTA Board and was an executive member of the YMCA as well as auxiliary president for two terms and on various fund-raising committees in other organizations. I was active in Republican politics and involved with Operation Eagle Eye, an organization that attempted to stop vote fraud at the voting booths in Chicago's inner city areas during the turbulent sixties. We were trained and went down in pairs to our stations early in the morning of election day. Warned against drinking the water and accepting food, we witnessed and recorded the attempted rigging of the machines and the illiterates being carried in to place an "X" by their names in exchange for a bottle of wine to get the Democrats in power. We were a block away from where Senator Charles Percy was assaulted. I was campaigning for him, as well as Senator Everett Dirkson and Congressman Donald Rumsfeld.

I had inexhaustible energy, and I didn't understand that it was all right to be still. To achieve, I thought I had to be busy. I was unaware of the value of wisdom and the quiet time often required to attain it. We rarely attended church as a family. I generally dropped the children off for Sunday school. I kept a poem above my desk entitled, "If He Came to Your House," and I never questioned but what that meant that our home had to be perfect. God would only enter a "perfect home." Everyone and everything in its place. We bred our new English springer spaniel, Ginger, and Barbie named her pick of the litter, Andrew, after her Grandfather's middle name. I loved my home and adored my husband and three children. I had so much—everything, some would say—and at five in the afternoon, I began to drink.

$\mathcal{P}$OWER AND STAFF

13

The cocktail hour was popular and acceptable during those years, and alcoholism was not discussed. Not the symptoms—not the treatments—not a hotline—not a commercial. I was a good person. Integrity, honesty and love for family and others were deeply important to me. It never occurred to me that the values I held dear were actually in danger of being overthrown. Women were expected to be able to drink and were given every opportunity under the sun, but as Betty Ford said so aptly, "They certainly were not expected to have a drinking problem." Why should I be any different?

Somewhere and somehow, I had lost the ability to reason. To think through to the consequences was not a part of my thought process, and I assumed I could handle anything. Certainly that was better than revealing weakness or risking rejection or judgments. I was a very good person who was very sick, and I didn't know how to get well because I didn't acknowledge even to myself that I was sick. The classic tale of *The Little Prince*[1] spoke for me:

"Why are you drinking?" demanded the little prince.
"So that I may forget," replied the tippler.
"Forget what?" inquired the little prince, who already was sorry for him.
"Forget that I am ashamed," the tippler confessed, hanging his head.
"Ashamed of what?" asked the little prince, who wanted to help him.
"Ashamed of drinking." The tippler brought his speech to an end and shut himself up in an impregnable silence.

Something evil was invading me that was too ugly to share. I was actually willing to suffer and deny at the same time. It was my private shame—repress it. Because it (temporarily) increased my ability to be supermom, alcohol had become my personal power. Because of my fierce independence and the preconceived idea that I could lean only on myself, self-reliance had become my staff.

I'd make myself a gin and tonic or whiskey sour. Bill would come home and mix a martini. One drink a night led to two per night while we sat in front of the fireplace in the soft white monotone living room talking about our day long after the children had eaten their dinner. As time went on, I'd hurry and make myself a second drink before he got home, and thinking it was my first, he'd make me another while fixing his second. I could hold the liquor well, and it continued to help me sleep. I had figured out my own unique strategies and the cycle was in motion. It was like being on a roller coaster in full gear that couldn't be stopped long after the ride was over. I wasn't aware of the dangerous medical problems developing inside of me. My tolerance of alcohol seemed almost supernatural, and after all, I had spent years hating what alcohol did to my mother. I'd never be like her—I couldn't be.

On one of his visits to our home, my father said to me one evening, "Karen, aren't you drinking a little too much?" *Why should he care?* I thought to myself. Everything was fine as usual. His question was the closest anyone came to confronting me about alcoholism for over twelve years. I began to increase my intake so that I wouldn't experience withdrawal. I felt more helpless as time went on. My honest and deep feelings seemed to be out of reach as if frozen by time.

Teenagers frightened me, or was I afraid of my shadow? I was trying so hard to maintain the perfect mom image—why was it so hard? I was unable to live up to the standard I had set for myself. Why was I failing? And what on earth was normal?

I began to have difficulty coping with the counterculture antics of one of the kids and I began to have trouble sleeping. I decided red wine would do the trick. We've all heard about wine being prescribed for relaxation, so after our late dinner, I poured myself a glass of Zinfandel. I sometimes kept a bottle under my bed, but being a lady, I always poured it into a small glass and set it on my night stand. The emotional war that was fighting inside me declared that it might be wiser to take sleeping pills. I asked our internist and he prescribed Placydil. He also sent me to a psychiatrist, who, after trying to interpret my dreams and attempting hypnosis, prescribed Thorazene and then Stelazine. Each one threw me into wild hallucinations, and I felt like a machine that couldn't be turned off. Even my eyelids fluttered uncontrollably. The walls around me were slanting and black things crawled up and down them, and they couldn't be caught. I panicked on the phone to the doctor, who said I was allergic to the "zenes" and he prescribed Librium to treat depression. I was never treated for alcoholism. If ever I was questioned by a physician as to

whether or not I drank, handled as a routine question ver-
sus a confrontation, I'd reply that I would have a couple of
cocktails with my husband every evening. Even with the
physicians' knowledge that some amount of alcohol was
being regularly consumed, the prescriptions continued. And
the drinking continued. It all became a challenge of skill—
a dangerous game, and I was the only one keeping the score.

S TUMBLING IN THE DARK
14

W e were in the painful sixties, a counterculture period that was alarmingly destructive for young people to be caught up in, and we had our own built-in humdinger. I was told, at one point, that she needed a closer mother-daughter relationship. I cared so deeply, yet I didn't know how to provide for all her needs—I could only guess.

There was one time when Julie was missing. She had just calmly walked out of the house on an unusually mild Sunday afternoon in November in her jeans and a shirt, carrying a light jacket, saying she was going to a friend's house down the street. Four days later, on Thanksgiving morning, she called to say she was coming home. When the police got to our house to wait for and question her, they told me that when they received my call saying she was safe, they were on their way into the city to check on a report that a girl had been found floating in the Chicago River who matched our daughter's description. I leaned against the wall of our entry as the police shared the information. A panicky fear had already threatened to cripple me. Now what? There didn't seem to be anything to hold me together. The reality of my feeling was that I was a failure; otherwise, why did this happen? And would it happen again? And then the sputtering engine in my head inwardly responded, *Put me in any situation and I will handle it—I won't feel—I'll take care of it because I cannot let it or myself get out of control.* It wasn't the first or the last frightening episode. She was safe this time, her family exhausted, and poor Julie had a mother who was losing her sanity.

The following Sunday morning after church, I shared a little of what happened with our minister, who answered, "I knew that kind of thing was apt to happen." He had never called on us, but knew our family through occasional church attendance and Julie through choir. My expectation was that he'd be sensitive to our need for support and guidance. We never heard from him. Too much for the minister, I suppose, but I wouldn't have felt so alone if he had just been willing to listen.

It was years later that Julie spoke poignantly about listening—we had listened to professionals about her problems, but we had not listened to *her.* She acted out because she thought that negative attention was better than none at all.

"Even though sober" does not mean that one is in her right mind! Alcohol has the ability to destroy one's mind—and not just during the period of active drinking. Alcohol combined with prescription drugs is a double whammy! The inability to actively and compassionately listen leads to misunderstandings and feelings of rejection.

I continued to trust the reputable doctors, who were supposed to know how to make me feel better. Instead, I was being treated with some drugs that had the same side effects as alcohol. I began to have chronic colon problems, and my back hurt when my stomach hurt. I became aware that I shouldn't talk on the telephone at night because my words were slurred. My judgment was becoming dulled. Progressively, I didn't say the things I meant and I didn't mean the things I said. I cried on the inside and felt like I was living in my own shadow that was clinging to me and becoming so dark that I couldn't find my way. So I drank. As devoted as I was to my husband and children, alcohol became a higher priority than family dynamics.

I was periodically having blackouts, and there was a time I found myself sitting in my car under an overpass and on the shoulder of the expressway between Northbrook and Chicago. It felt like I woke up there. But I didn't know why I was there or where I was going or where I was coming from. I never told anyone because they might have thought I was crazy, and I was too frightened to want to know if that was true.

After collapsing in my doctor's office one day, I was hospitalized, and after many tests, diabetes mellitus was diagnosed and I was put on Orinase and a strict bland diet. I was also on birth control pills and Tincture of Bella Donna, Librium and Viokase. I continued to take iron for anemia and large doses of prescribed vitamin E as a dietary supplement. Darvon didn't work, so a tiny pill was prescribed to place under my tongue for extreme colon pain that would be gone by the time the pill dissolved.

I was generally quiet at social functions, having had at least one drink with a Librium to calm my nerves before we left for a dinner party or fund-raising dance. I'd have an acceptable number of drinks at the event, knowing that there was plenty more at home where I'd be able to finish the evening along with a Placydil and a glass or two of Zinfandel. Very rarely was I out of control, but there were occasions where I knew that I slurred my words and repeated myself, dropped food or drink on my dress, and one time I ripped my blue satin gown. I learned many years later that I also cried whenever asked about our older daughter, that I gave an inappropriate toast at a wedding, and that I danced half naked on the sofa in the home of friends. I was thin, my eyes were puffy, and I was nutritionally unsound. My fingers and toes were tingling, and I remembered my mother complaining about that. But I was too frightened to say a word. I didn't eat sweets or even want them. I was getting enough sugar from the alcohol. I didn't fit the stereotype of the impoverished, immoral, skid row woman, and I didn't go to bars. I had a good figure, my stomach wasn't bloated and I wasn't bruised. I tried my best to not let others see me or hear me when I had too much to drink—after all, I was a nice lady with proper social graces. I wasn't beaten with my husband's belt, and I didn't crawl on the hallway floor, and I didn't threaten anyone with a knife. But I was my mother's daughter. And I was just as sick as she was and getting sicker. I was losing my way.

We drank for joy and became miserable.
We drank for sociability and became argumentative.
We drank for sophistication and became obnoxious.
We drank for friendship and made enemies.
We drank for sleep and awakened exhausted.
We drank to diminish our problems and saw them multiply.
We drank for strength and felt weak.
We drank to feel exhilaration and ended up depressed.
We drank for "medicinal" purposes and acquired health problems.
We drank to get calmed down and ended up with the shakes.
We drank for confidence and became afraid.
*We drank to make conversation flow easily and the words came
out incoherently.*
We drank to feel heavenly and ended up feeling like hell.
We drank to cope with life and invited hell.

Author unknown

$\mathcal{H}$ELPLESSNESS REIGNS
15

$\mathcal{B}$ill's wonderful mother suddenly died at age sixty-three. I adored her and could never understand why Bill married me. I was definitely not like the girl that married dear ole dad. She wasn't complicated—not the handful that I was.

My Uncle Ernie was dying of cancer. He and Mama Hon had moved to Milwaukee, which was closer to us and not a bad drive on the expressway. He had become the Grand Secretary of the Masonic Lodge for the State of Wisconsin, and like the rest of the family, I was proud of his achievements. Little did I realize that the Masons were considered close to being a cult with their mysterious closed-door secret meetings. I gathered some bright yellow daffodils from our garden one morning, took a Librium and drove to the hospital. I knew I was seeing him for the last time and tried to express my love and gratitude for the wonderful memories he and Mama Hon had given me, for making it feel easy to be part of their family when times were especially hard. I drove home to Northbrook that evening with childlike tears and pictures of yesterday in my mind as I remembered my uncle being the one real man who held me on his lap when I was a little girl. And he was soon to die. It was five o'clock, and I mixed a martini.

I was beginning to feel like a body with no one at home inside. Reasoning power and a clear awareness of life around me, the ability to seek wisdom and solid direction all seemed far beyond my grasp. I looked at myself as a failure and a complete mistake—but not ready to give up. The alcohol and my addiction to prescription drugs were helping to cut off my feelings—the ones that I most needed to deal with—they were becoming trapped in a pool of infection. I couldn't believe that my mask was so effective that even our doctor wouldn't say something to me. Since he hadn't, I continued to move as fast as I could, drink as much as I needed, and take as many pills as I thought my body could tolerate to keep me functioning. Scrambled messages in my brain were telling me that I hated myself, and my shame became almost unbearable—at the same time I was under the impression I was strong enough to take all the abuse. I was too frightened to believe otherwise.

Our two younger children, seven and fourteen years of age, were experiencing bronchial asthma so frequently and ferociously that it was suggested by their pediatrician that I take them to the desert area for the long winter months; however, Bill wouldn't allow the family to be separated, so in 1969 we prepared again to move to southern California. We left the windy city that held a part of my childhood and growing up years; the light of the beacon on the Palmolive Building that had been a reminder of something constant and beautiful; happy years and others beaten down by tragedy, uncertainty and fear. I would miss Chicago and our Northbrook friends and community. I'd not miss the flat countryside, the electrical storms or the increasingly terrifying tornadoes. Freak weather conditions added to my fears.

As we drove away from our home, I remembered the afternoon in early spring when the sky became green. The air was thick and still. Warnings of a funnel sighted came over the radio and Barbie and David were hustled into the basement with the dog, as I drove to the high school to get Julie. On our way back home, Julie said, "Look in back, Mom!" We saw the roof of the gymnasium being lifted off the building. I drove faster. Bill was out of town that week, so he also missed the big storm after the tornado when lightning struck and sliced the tree outside the kitchen window, and we all camped out in the basement without power and phone. I'd be happy to leave all that behind. I redirected my thoughts to California. To improved health for the children in the dry sunshine surrounded by mountains of beauty and the Pacific Ocean.

Two years later, and seven years after my mother's death, my father was dying of cancer of the liver. He had been ill for just six weeks, and it was February when Bill and I flew to Chicago. He was very jaundiced when we saw him, and from his hospital bed he told me he was sorry that he hadn't been a better father. I knew he had done his best. I had always accepted that as fact. There was no more depth or gentleness than that between us—as there never had been—and we left another winter death behind with skeleton trees scratching the heavy gray sky.

*T*HE BALANCING ACT

16

*B*ill was employed again in the trade show industry, and the children's health was dramatically improved. We lived in our dream house on two acres in Yorba Linda and were members of the Balboa Bay Club on the ocean, where we kept a small blue and white Dolphin sailboat. We had a riding horse and a lamb that ate ivy, six laying hens and geese, dogs and cats and a rabbit. We gathered eggs and picked oranges off our trees each morning for a healthy breakfast. I helped David reach high into the avocado trees for the fruit that he'd take to the packing house to be weighed and sold. He was in Cub Scouts and I the den mother. He played in Little League where his lifelong passion for baseball began, and we loved to share in his fun. And I drank and took pills. Valium had replaced Librium when we moved to the west coast.

Thinking there must be a marital problem, I sought guidance from our minister at the Community Church, who invited Bill to join me for group marriage rap sessions. I recall sitting in the pastor's office one morning when I noticed a Bible heaped on top of a pile of books on the floor next to my chair. I quickly and reverently placed it on the table instead. The pastor told me something about how we're not to worship the *book* but to *use* it to know God's Word and to worship *Him*.

It was a tumultuous time in the life of our older daughter, who decided at eighteen that it was time for her to leave home, and she had our blessing. Julie moved back to the Chicago area where she eventually married. Though she was to become a wonderful wife and mother of two, my attempt at being the perfect mom hadn't worked, and I blamed only myself for my daughter's unhappiness in an imperfect home. I went to a psychologist in Whittier once a week for over a year to get help in figuring me out. I was so confused and anxious that I took a couple of Valium to help me function behind the wheel and calm my nerves so that I could explain my feelings to him. I was also on Librax now for my colon discomfort.

Barbie was in high school and a foreign exchange student from Germany came to live with us for six months. Shortly after we moved in and bought a Morgan gelding horse that Barbie rode bareback, I left for a political luncheon only to return and find that the pasture gate had been left open after a hay delivery. With no horse in sight and no experience in handling him, I began running across the field of lavender lupines in my heels and beige silk dress. Four "blocks" later, in a paved residential area, I saw the giant brown animal near a milk delivery truck. I took off my shoes and ran down the hill. "See that horse?" I called. The driver held onto him for me and said that leading him by the mane wouldn't hurt. Irish Red and I came to understand one another, and he was very gentle and patient with me from that time on.

The horse and the lamb were good friends. Barbie and her boyfriend periodically took the lamb in Jim's truck to get it sheared at the high school agricultural department. When they returned Maggie to the corral one day after she had been shorn to within an inch of her life, Irish Red gaped at her, then threw his head back with mouth open wide showing all teeth, and gave the biggest horse laugh we'd ever seen. Poor embarrassed Maggie scooted into a corner under a tree to sulk a while before taking her favorite position under all fours of her usually protective friend.

After moving to Yorba Linda, I alternately attended the Methodist and the Presbyterian churches. Bill had been raised in a "Christian" home, and regular church attendance was a part of their lives as were the youth activities that he participated in for most of his growing up years. Because of that, it was hard for me to understand why he chose to sleep in on Sunday mornings. I knew he worked hard and it was his only morning to relax. I also had always imagined, although we never discussed it, that his sense of stability and goodness was derived from his religious beliefs and background that included attending church.

One of my community activities was volunteering my time at Children's Hospital. I marveled at the courage of five-year-old Diana who suffered from Cystic Fibrosis. And I wept for the beautiful four-month-old baby girl who had been physically abused by her parents. The only time she slept was when she was not touched. As soon as hands reached into her crib to change or lift her, big brown eyes flashed open wide and kept their gaze. I never heard her cry. I held her in the rocking chair while she took her bottle, and I sang lullabies to this innocent little child whose eyes didn't close until placed back in the crib and left alone.

I was a Board member of the hospital guild and loved the social life, though at no time did it come close to touching my heart as did the children whose future was painfully uncertain. I was becoming very fearful of my own health but was even more afraid to tell anyone. When I lifted a small child who depended upon my strength to hold it, fear and anxiety overtook me. Shaking from Valium and Placydil and the other prescriptions in combination with whiskey and wine from the night before, I was so out of balance that I felt unable to hold a tiny, fragile life. Unable to explain my reasons, I left the volunteer program.

*F*RAGILE CHAMELEON
17

I went to Carmel in northern California for a business and social weekend with Bill. There was a Pebble Beach golf tournament for many of the celebrities, and President and Mrs. Ford attended. I had no idea how deeply into her multiple addictions Betty Ford was at the time. A pretty woman, she also had the look of an unreal but coping presence with which I could easily identify. My abdomen hurt all of the time. I couldn't sit upright in the car or at a table for very long, and I was unable to wear a tight belt. I used my heating pad as much as possible and took my prescribed drugs including Lomotyl for ongoing diarrhea. I tried hard to not complain and continued to be *fine*. After a weekend of partying, I had to lie down flat on the back seat as Bill and I drove the six hours home that Sunday night. After some medical tests, diverticulitis of the transverse colon was diagnosed.

We enjoyed the Bay Club where we swam and played tennis, had saunas, and sailed the Dolphin. In the evening, we occasionally had a few drinks in the lounge as Ron Brown played the piano before we left for home. One time Bill and I took separate cars, and on that night, Barbie chose to return home with me. She asked me to let her drive. "Of course not!" I could certainly manage. She was frightened as we drove the winding road through parts of Irvine. I'd show her I could do it. Suddenly, a car with an elderly couple pulled abruptly over to the shoulder and waited until we passed. Startled, I watched out of the rear view mirror as I slowed and steadied the old T-bird the best I could. I remember the curious thought in my head, *People do that only when they see drunk drivers!* I may have been drinking, but I couldn't imagine that I, Karen, could be drunk. That hideous word couldn't describe *me.* I very seldom drove freeways after that. Everywhere I went in southern California was to be traveled on back roads where I could go slow and not draw attention and not concern anyone else. I responded to questioning friends and family that they were missing beautiful scenery by driving on the freeways.

I worked hard for the Yorba Linda Service League and enjoyed the various roles on the Board. Bill and I entertained frequently and hosted business functions, a large wedding reception for a community leader, political events, fund-raising luncheons and dinners, and we attended gala events in Los Angeles. And I was getting weaker and feeling more helpless as drinking and prescription drugs manipulated and advanced my chameleon behavior. Barbie Anne was married, and her wedding in Laguna Beach was perfection. After the first two hours of the dinner dance reception, I was unable to recall a single moment of the evening. Nothing that happened was stored in my brain— therefore, nothing to be recalled. It was one of my many blackouts.

I was asked to develop a volunteer service program for our brand-new community hospital. I plunged right in to

organize a *super* successful project. I loved the opportunity
and the people I worked with and gave to the max to make
it a model program for North Orange County. I trained and
supervised over two hundred volunteers (not including the
gift shop), designed and wrote the procedure booklet, attended seminars in Orange and Los Angeles counties, initi-
ated special programs within programs such as blood
replacement, and helped in public relations. The single area
I consciously and unconsciously avoided was anything to
do with pastoral visitation. But I did notice the elderly volunteer as she carried her Bible into the rooms of patients.
She had asked me for permission. I sometimes wondered
what she said to the sick, but I never asked her. I took Valium
on a regular basis and doubled the dose prior to giving a
daytime orientation or other presentation. Before conduct-
ing evening orientations, I'd go home and have vodka drinks
with dinner so there wouldn't be liquor on my breath. Then
I'd take another Valium and return to the hospital.

In 1973, I required a hysterectomy. I fought the anes-
thetic, and I was told later that my garbled talk in recovery
was "very interesting." I was removed from a double room
because of extreme discomfort and given privacy as I tried
to recover, while hoping no one would suspect that I was
experiencing hallucinations. It was not my first major surgery, and it was not to be my last. It was the most difficult
because of my multiple addiction that was my toxic shame.
Though I felt much loved and respected by the volunteers
and staff, I was too fearful of returning to the program, terrified of being confronted, rejected, judged without mercy.
Or was I the one guilty of judging myself so mercilessly?

STORMS OF FEARS
18

Our son was doing exceptionally well in a private
school, and I began to help Bill in the exhibit business. Something I was never going to do. My mother did
that, and I was not going to be like her. I was not going to
live in confusion and with progressive insanity. I was not
going to be the victim of an evil controlling power that
could make me different and sick. I worked in public relations, designed brochures and letterheads, and, like my
parents, we took clients out for lunch and that invariably
meant one or two martinis first. I went to a few conventions in the area on my own and attended a Christian book
show where I heard Katherine Marshall speak. I thought
she was wonderful.

Although I had brief periods of abstinence from alcohol, nothing removed the static going on inside. I was dis-
oriented at night and early morning when it became
increasingly difficult to wake up, and I continued to experience frightening hallucinations. I didn't feel safe in my
world, yet I was unable to escape. Truth could hardly be

tolerated. The hand tremors that hindered my writing were frequent and my vision was blurred. I had trouble with my equilibrium and had difficulty walking in my own home when not drinking. I needed to use a cart to lean on in the grocery store even if there for just a stick of butter. I felt safer in a crowd than with much space around me—that gave me the sense of suspension. I experienced shortness of breath and wondered what caused the heart palpitations. I had rheumatic fever as a child that left me with a heart murmur. My doctor wasn't overly concerned and gave me a prescription. I had long memory gaps and increasing black-outs. Because of colitis, it had been a very long time since I'd been able to tolerate cold orange juice in the morning or milk at any time. The heating pad soothed my aching abdomen. I was taking Orinase, Lomotyl, Valium, Librax and Placydil regularly.

Giants of fears plagued me: an inner panic of seeing a fire on television; building a fire in the fireplace; visualizing both helplessness and power in the kitchen drawer of knives that reminded me of the closet episode with my mother; the sensation of wanting to open the car door on the freeway when Bill was driving; fear of open spaces and the fear of being suspended and out of control when crossing an intersection by car or by foot; escalators and marbled floors; bad dreams and nightmares. I'd say to myself, *There's nothing to fear but fear itself,* but they wouldn't go away, so I'd make the determination that I must be losing my sanity after all. *But please don't let that be true.*

In addition to martinis, scotch or vodka beginning at five o'clock most evenings, we frequently had an after dinner liqueur. Bill kept a large inventory and enjoyed being able to serve an assortment to guests. A couple of drinks relaxed him and helped our communication—why was I

so different? Why did I have to sneak and hide in our bedroom and bath later? Why did I have to pretend? *What was
wrong with me that it affected me so differently?*

I liked to read in bed, and as soon as Bill was asleep, I'd
pour myself another glass of wine. I took a Placydil and
poured a little more wine before turning out the light. I
often woke up after only a few hours of sleep, thinking I
must not have taken my pill. I fumbled around for one or
two more. I couldn't remember—I didn't know I was a
chemical time bomb. No one had told me about the fatal
complications that could occur because of my cross tolerance. It was difficult to even consider a serious drug addiction when those very drugs were prescribed by my
physician. Valium was one that made me think I was doing
well when I was really failing. I had the vague sense that I
was overdosing while I was feeding myself the unknown
quantities of pills and drinks; however, there were two sides
of the familiar conflict battling within. One side argued,
"Her body can take it—look how much she's consumed in
the past and nothing has happened—her prescriptions continue to get refilled, and no one has confronted her, so they
must think she can handle it." While the other side quietly
and limply replied, "She really cannot take much more, and
she's almost beyond caring, so watch it!"

Like my mother, I was also addicted to smoking. I was
going through almost a pack of cigarettes a day even though
I had attempted to stop many times, and I knew how upset
it made David, in particular, to see me smoke. He was the
boy who had recently said, "Mom, I never promised you a
rose garden," as he dug the planting holes along our sunny
driveway. And he made me a wonderful card that said I
deserved the best-mother-in-the-world award. I was so
thankful he didn't know that I felt like I should be below
the grave of the earth.

Patterns

David was thirteen that year, and we put him on a plane bound for summer camp. Unknown to him, I was making plans to drive to Solvang, a Danish community northeast of Santa Barbara the following day, and I was not intending to return home. I told Bill that I needed to be completely away "for a while," and I put a small suitcase in my car. I had made reservations at a motel where I anticipated making the decision to either end my life or to disappear into the world and become a nonperson. I was tired of twelve and a half years of pain that wouldn't go away. I was weary of the consequences of failure. I had failed to save my mother, and I had let Julie down. My husband and children suffered because of my failures and shameful afflictions. I couldn't even save myself—but I hadn't died yet . . .

My children meant the world to me, and I could hardly stand the thought of not being there for them. At the same time, my irrational mind reasoned that anyone else could be a better mother for them, and they deserved to be taken care of in a "normal" environment. I didn't know that suicide was considered a sin. I felt like a vicious storm was blowing around in my mind—fears tossed to and fro that constantly threatened to defy my making healthy choices— that threatened to paralyze my ability to reason. The agony of my mind confused my plans, and I was losing my grasp of any hope at all. I loved my family, but I couldn't let my life damage the ones I cared about the most. Nor did I want my death to be their pain. I was trying to hold on to my dreams when I felt like I was losing my soul.

I am more powerful
than the combined armies of the world
I have destroyed more men
than all the wars of the nation
I have caused millions of accidents and wrecked more homes
than all the floods, tornadoes and hurricanes put together
I am the world's slickest thief
I steal billions of dollars each year
I find my victims among the rich and poor alike
the young and the old, the strong and the weak
I loom up to such proportions that I cast a shadow
over every field of labor
I am relentless, insidious, unpredictable;
I am everywhere—in the home, on the street,
in the factory, in the office
on the sea and in the air
I bring sickness, poverty and death
I give nothing and take all
I am your worst enemy
I am alcohol

Author unknown

MIRACLE—CUSTOM DESIGNED
19

The day after David left for camp, I was sitting in my T-bird in the driveway of our Yorba Linda home with a pad of paper and pencil next to me to record my thoughts as I drove. Along with the Valium I had taken and the supply I had with me, writing would help to divert my fears of driving such a distance on the freeway. It puzzled me to suddenly feel an urge to run back in the house for two specific items. One was my King James Bible that I hadn't looked at since a small child with my grandmother. The other was the small, red leather edition of Norman Vincent Peale's book, *The Power of Positive Thinking*[2] that I had salvaged from the Chicago brownstone where my mother had died years earlier. I placed them on the seat, and trying not to look back at my home in the bright sunshine of a smog-free morning, I pulled away.

About four hours later, I arrived in Solvang and drove through the town, spotting the liquor store that I'd return to after unpacking. I drove on to the Meadowlark Motel that was rather isolated on the outskirts of the village, and

I noticed a church situated on either side. There was a Seventh Day Adventist and a Baptist church. My room was number twelve on the Baptist side. I had loved coming to Solvang with the family. With its

The Meadowlark Motel – 1915 – Solvang

old world charm and softness of spirit, it now seemed the perfect place for a retreat, for anonymity to begin, even for finality.

I hung up a few clothes and was preparing to go out again when I looked down on the table by the door where I had placed my Bible and my mother's book. I decided to sit for a minute, still curious as to why I brought these, and I opened the books. I began to read them alternately with a hunger I couldn't understand. And I couldn't leave the room . . .

Dr. Peale said to read Matthew 17:20 about having faith as small as a mustard seed, and Romans 8:31, "If God be for us, who can be against us?" I was astonished to read that perfect peace comes when resting our mind upon God. I forgot about why I was in Solvang. I forgot about going back out to the liquor store. I continued to read into the night in the little motel room.

Philippians 4:13, "I can do all things through Christ who strengtheneth me." Dr. Peale wrote of the value of child-like faith. Of being renewed. And to be of good courage and not afraid because "the Lord my God would be with me and never forsake me," as in Deuteronomy 31:6. Then Dr. Peale spoke of the heart and I understood him to mean that if I very simply opened my heart to God, the rest would follow. I didn't have to be concerned about knowledge and skill. The emphasis was on the heart.

With the tiniest grain of a mustard seed faith, based upon God's promises I had just read, I fell onto the bed and cried out to God with all my heart. I told Him I wanted to live, but I couldn't do it alone—I told Him how much I hated myself, that I couldn't stand myself any longer—that I wanted His peace and His strength—I asked Him to please help me—to please heal me and make me new—to please come into my heart—please give me life as He wanted it to be—I belong to Him.

I slowly felt the presence of God in that room. The atmosphere was heavy and it was safe. It was powerful and it was secure. I felt as though I were in a cocoon of complete love and unconditional compassion. There was a deep, heart-knowing presence. Something new and wonderfully comforting. I felt the protection of God, and I fell into a peaceful and sound sleep.

I awoke a few hours later and it was a whole new morning. I was amazed at how refreshed and vital I seemed from the inside out—really glad to be alive—clean—in tune with God—with a beginning hold on truth—an enthusiasm for being. His perfect love gave me an awareness and assurance that with God I would forever feel that love, even during times when I had no other feeling.

I showered and dressed and walked out onto the rolling countryside. I came upon a small forest and took a path that led to a little glen that was surrounded by lush green ferns and a high rocky cliff ahead. I looked up to see a beautiful rainbow and my heart felt a belonging to God. I didn't know at the time that the rainbow is a sign of God's covenant with us.

Later that afternoon of July 7, 1975, I drove into town for dinner. I hadn't eaten since the morning before and I was suddenly starved for a smorgasbord at the Molenkroen restaurant where we had gone as a family. I hurried up the steep stairs of the old building and was seated at a small table near the railing. The meal was wonderful as always, but then the traditional complimentary cherry liqueur was set in front of me. I didn't know what I should do. I hadn't thought about it—maybe it won't hurt me anymore—or maybe it would, and I shouldn't drink it. Old reasoning and habit patterns came into play, and I raised the cordial halfway to my lips, when, suddenly, I was compelled to look about fifteen feet away and next to a post. Christ Jesus was there. I couldn't take my eyes off Him, and I remember wondering if others could see Him. His presence was lifelike in  size and alive in Spirit. His form was concealed in a translucent robe of purple, golden, silver green and crimson—softly draped. His face was not visible. I felt the magnitude of His power which equaled the sight of Jesus. A magical light that illuminated a spellbinding presence that overwhelmed and consumed my entire being, as if nothing else in all the world mattered. That was the Glory of Jesus Christ as I saw Him.

I have no idea how long He was there—seconds or minutes—it was during that limitless time that Christ removed all my desire for alcohol! He set me free and gave me an assurance that He was surrounding me with His protective shield to carry for the rest of my life. I had received a miracle of healing. The old was gone. I was a new creature and instantly healed of alcoholism by the living Christ. Isaiah 9:2 says that "the people who walk in darkness have seen a great light," and it was He who turned my darkness into light, and Isaiah 61:10 says how "He clothed me with garments of salvation." I knew that Christ had given me everything I needed for a new life and it was a gift that could never be taken away. I had felt the majesty of His power as I had seen His glory!

One of the first things I did was to write Julie and ask for her forgiveness. I shared what had happened to me, and my prayer was that she be healed of the pain that had been caused by my affliction, that bad memories also would be healed and that her own heart would be softened.

Bill spent the following weekend with me in Solvang. I wanted to show him where "my" rainbow had arched its colors and the exact place where Christ had chosen to heal me of alcoholism. I remained in the Danish village for another week to try to absorb all that had happened. I bought a few art supplies and sketched some of the beauty of the landscape that I hiked for miles around in the sunshine of July.

I began to communicate daily with the Lord on a personal level that led me to feel loved and deeply connected to Him. I felt fully alive—cleansed and free. A crushing evil had pulled me off balance and had come close to taking my life, yet God "saw my affliction and knew the anguish of my soul," as in Psalm 31, and He desired to reveal to me His amazing grace. It is said that the greatest miracle is the conversion of the human soul. I believe it!

My heart touched His . . . with childlike faith, I sought to kneel on the palm of His hand . . . He responded to the cry of my soul, the very thing He had created . . . Truth was not in hiding . . . It is my heart-knowing that He healed me to win my soul and to see Christ Jesus as Someone Real.

$\mathcal{P}$ATTERN OF CHANGE
20

I've come to believe that for the ones who yearn for God, He does for us what we simply cannot do—by the same token, He does not do for us what we can do. Who prayed for me? One person or many? Why was I allowed to suffer so long? Did *anyone* pray for me? What about the multiple addiction and, because of it, the physical and mental abuse my body had endured for that period? What all *does* God do—and what does He expect from me?

People suffering from alcoholism are usually extremely sensitive and insightful. Loneliness is very real to those who grow up in a world of pretend—who've not had the security of sharing their own individuality. Starving for truth was what made me persevere and also what made me want to run away.

I probably won't know until I see Christ in heaven why He miraculously heals some and not others, but I have a few ideas.

It was the only way He could bring me to my knees before Him. I didn't knowingly reject Him all those years of growing up and beyond. Like my mother, helplessness and fear had created a vacuum that became so contaminated, I was absolutely blinded. I think I really was searching for many years for something very special to fill the deep need of my heart.

He knew that I had to have a crisis experience in order to believe my transformation.

He knew that I would share my experiences and spiritual journey in speaking, in hospital volunteer work and in writing. I had to have credibility so that others would understand my reason for trust and hope in Him.

He has also always known that I will not place a moral judgment on people who suffer from the disease.

I had twelve and a half years of alcoholism. Longer than some, not nearly as long as others. I was very sick, yet not as acutely ill as the alcoholics who never leave the hospital intensive care unit. There are Christians as well as non-Christians who endure the agony of this misunderstood disease. And there but by the grace of God go any one of us.

The light of the Chicago beacon has been showing the way to the lost for as long as I can remember. But the light of Christ has *always* been there. As wonderful as that is, to reflect on that truth gives me a sense of sadness because of all the years I could have known Him and didn't. It's as though I was blind for forty-three years—lost in patterns of darkness. It reminds me of the spiritual, "Amazing Grace" and how "I once was lost, but now I'm found, was blind, but now I see."

In John 12:35, Jesus said, "Walk while you have the light, so that the darkness may not overtake you. If you walk in the darkness, you do not know where you are going." The promises of God are to be taken seriously. The fact that He has the supernatural power to heal needs to be accepted.

It's been over seventeen years since July 7, 1975, and not once have I been tempted by alcohol. I didn't know He would do that. I just asked for help after coming to the end of myself and humbly sought to be His child.

The disease that almost destroyed me without my knowing it can be compared to a melanoma on one's back that others can see as it gets larger and darker, but the victim is oblivious until it's almost too late. Treatment is essential; just as cancer and heart disease are life-threatening, so is alcoholism, which is regarded by many to be the number one killer in America today. Yet 84 percent of alcoholic patients will recover if forced into or given treatment at any stage!

As my father had been with my mother, my husband was in denial for the duration of my illness. Patterns repeat themselves in many significant ways from generation to generation. It took me a long time to get over the resentments and justifiable anger, particularly because of the pain that had rested unnecessarily on our children. Why do I say that? Some will express amazement when the spouse hangs in there—they think we're lucky when that happens. Maybe so; however, it's sacrificial love when the spouse is willing to change his or her lifestyle and tackle the problem head on when it's a matter of not only recovery for the alcoholic but improved health for the entire family.

Forgiveness is God's instrument to bring about reconciliation and inner peace. The reward is in knowing Jesus Christ, and that far exceeds suffering for any amount of time—to not know Him is to not know life. To not know the Lord separates us from His divine goodness and mercy forever. To not know Him is the ultimate of permanent darkness. There are worse things in life than alcoholism, cancer, AIDS or Alzheimer's, leprosy or starvation—to not know Christ is to live without hope and eternal security— to not know Christ is never to have a glimpse of God.

Christ is worth knowing at any cost! He gave me a sense of purpose. A source of wisdom. My protector. I hear it said frequently, "I don't know what people do who don't rely upon the Lord," especially in tragic circumstances. I remember what it was like. I used to panic instead of pray. I made choices without seeking God's direction. I depended upon man to meet my needs. I let fears cripple me rather than trust God. I tried to be a supermom when all I needed to do was to let Christ be the center of our home. I had no knowledge of the consequences of choosing to lean on self rather than give my burdens to the Lord. Dependence on my own strength gave me a false sense of security, and I was lonely, and really alone, in my unbelief.

*T*HE GIFT OF FAITH
21

I sang the hymns I remembered from my childhood on the way home to Yorba Linda—"Onward Christian Soldiers" and "Jesus Loves Me"—Jesus, who took me safely back on the freeway to my family and friends.

I shared my experience with my forever friend Susie, who listened and who understood. She gave me a small, powder blue Bible to carry with me everywhere and said I should write the names of the people I was praying for on the inside cover, then make a check mark when the prayer was answered. I called Lorraine who told me about Bible Study Fellowship. I wrote to Dr. Norman Vincent Peale, who included my story briefly in his next book.[3] I wanted to climb to the top of our roof like the fiddler and sing my message to a world of open ears. This gift of faith was taking over my life!

Bill began to go to church with me, and one Sunday morning, the request was made for a temporary home for a Vietnamese family of six who had been airlifted to Camp Pendleton. We immediately volunteered our home and prepared for a new kind of adventure. Although it was against my nature to turn away from a need, I would have been too frightened to take on that responsibility when under the influence of alcohol. Now I didn't have to think about sneaking a drink, taking a bottle to our bedroom or my slurred speech. I could talk on the phone at night and make plans. I could behave like a "normal" woman and create a "normal" environment for this needy family.

Because I did continue to have difficulty driving and trouble with hand tremors and other withdrawal symptoms, without my telling her the reasons, a friend drove me to pick up our refugees. Miles of golden brown tents, khaki uniforms and Vietnamese of all ages and sizes swarmed the dusty fields in sharp contrast to the clear blue shimmering Pacific Ocean across the highway. The mother and her five children were waiting for us at the Red Cross station.

Christine had given her family American first names on board the plane. She liked the beautiful sounds and she wanted to be American. Unable to speak English, they were nevertheless educated and appealing because they were so willing to adapt to our culture. We were to learn that they had lived in a villa in Saigon—the husband and father was a captain in the army, who was shot and killed one day as he was getting into his car outside of their home. Within two days, Christine paid the Saigonese government twenty thousand dollars—"cheap freedom" she called it—and with her children and as much jade as they could all wear, the family boarded the plane for the USA. It was impossible to imagine—losing one's husband, or father, followed by the loss of home and country, then getting accustomed to a new culture in a foreign land with strangers. We never heard a complaint or saw self-pity from this remarkable family.

The kids swam in the pool, ate corn-on-the-cob and chicken drumsticks, hamburgers, too, once Jan decided she wasn't allergic to red meat after all. They sunbathed, and Kathy Clairol-rinsed her shiny black hair with auburn high-lights, and they watched our home movies with glee.

Lisa was the oldest at nineteen and loved to paint with bright oils; Jan at seventeen did beautiful embroidery; Kathy, fifteen, enjoyed playing our piano. Six-year-old Paula had fun playing with the dolls I had saved, and little John, age four, loved having our David's attention whether by tying his shoes or reading a story.

We took our Vietnamese family to the Methodist Church with us every Sunday, after raising the American flag in our front yard and saying the Pledge of Allegiance. From the beginning of their two months with us, we learned how to communicate by expression and touch, love and much humor. And I thanked God every night for healing me of alcoholism. I was so excited to be able to begin thinking clearly. I was so thrilled to know who is strong when I am weak, who is in control, and who saves. I was ecstatic to learn that I could measure truth by the word of God.

In November of that year of '75, Bill and I went to a business convention and, during the first cocktail party of the evening, I was asked what kind of drink I'd like by one of the associates. "Any soft drink would be fine," I replied. "What's the matter; you don't drink?" the man asked. I told him "No, I've had a problem with alcohol, and I don't drink at all anymore." I still remember the look on his face when he said, "I wish I could say that." Later in the evening when others were laughing too loud and swaying too much as they walked, I felt almost giddy with delight that I could be having such a wonderful time without a drop of alcohol. In contrast with the others the next morning, I'd also remember everything that had been said the night before. I was having fun being free, and I liked me.

To my doctor's amazement and that of the insurance company, the diabetes mellitus was gone. My addiction to Valium left immediately, but other prescriptions took its place, and, in addition, I was having withdrawal symptoms and would be experiencing a medication imbalance for years to come. Physical consequences had taken their toll; emotional complications and painful memories can also last a long time even for those who are fortunate to receive treatment.

To begin to think and to respond clearly was a gift, and it has become my awareness that God meant for the rest of my healing to go slow and deep, equal to the growth of my faith. I've appreciated the analogy of the Monterey cypress, whose roots go deeper when the winds are strong—"down deep beneath the surface where faith grabs hold—where the water of God's Word feeds hope and reassurance."[4]

The diverticulitis of the transverse colon had advanced as far as possible without my needing major surgery. Librium and Librax, Premarin and Synthroid and a variety of sleeping pills continued to fill my medicine cabinet. At the same time, I began to take papaya enzymes and drink papaya juice to help my digestive system. No coconut, nuts or berries. I was going to be healthy! And while Bill continued his martini habit, I enjoyed having a glass of iced tea in the evening. I was learning what it was like to feel good. Formerly under the guise of the superwoman syndrome and my multiple addictions, everything outside of myself had become a cause. I had felt that it was selfish of me to spend time taking care of my own needs. That seemed self-seeking, and I couldn't tolerate that attitude. Until my life was on the line and God took over, I didn't understand or accept the fact that I was a valuable human being, and in order to be able to give all that He desired, it was imperative that I take care of myself in a manner pleasing to Him. I had a lot to learn. But God is a God of new beginnings, and I had been given the chance to help design new patterns.

Life Is an Adventure
22

Business circumstances changed drastically, and in 1977, Bill accepted a wonderful position in Oregon. It had been a childhood dream of his to someday settle in the Pacific Northwest, and it was easy for me to claim Portland as my new home. Surrounded by rivers with silver bridges and mountains of splendor, hills of fir trees and the ocean spreading from rocky cliffs not far from us, I fell in love with beauty all over again. I look at this part of the land as God's promise to the world that heaven is gentle.

Our funny little house on the lake had been built as a summer cottage, so it was cold and drafty in the winter, but the view from our sunroom at any time of year was what I wanted to look at until I died. A blue heron looked like a spindly old man as he stood on the dock. When he took off, his wings opened with ease and grace while he gently glided over the still water. Gray moods were just as natural as brilliant blue-green, and the white caps were an occasional surprise. Our end of the lake was quiet—the swish and roar of water skis and power boats were in the distance. We sailed the blue Dolphin and watched the sun rise . . . firs and willows owned the shoreline, gardens of roses, pink rhododendrons and iris, wide green lawns . . . and after the rain with the gleam of the sun, rainbows— sometimes double—reached for gold across the lake of my borrowed dreams. Chicago seemed very far away.

We moved Andrew, our springer, Annie the calico cat and honey-toned Frazier, who resembled the lion as he stretched and surveyed the new territory. Oregon skies have fluffy white clouds that remind me of Wisconsin lambs and children playing. Beautiful Andrew, with thick wavy fur, was getting old. He spent more time watching the mallards with glistening emerald backs than chasing them. He loved going out in the boat, but it broke our hearts to see less spring in his steps as he began to miss the leap from the dock. He reminded me a little of Lady dog in La Crosse, who used to howl in tune with the sirens. Andrew just sat by the lake with black and white head held high as he listened to the drifting sound of his own voice.

Our daughters were happily married with babies on the way, and David—who had become a Christian the year after I did—was away at school. I enjoyed painting again and took a sculpture class. I was led to a Bible Study in a new friend's home and learned from the "pros" ways in which to study God's Word. I had never seen people write in their Bibles, and I had an awful time spelling Isaiah and remembering the order of the books. Fears and lack of trust had patterned my life for so long that I hesitated telling my friends that the first time I read through the Book of Revelation, I had nightmares. And I finally grasped who in heaven's name was the Holy Ghost!

We found a new church, and after a conversation with the pastor, I found myself speaking to a large women's group about the miracle God had performed in my life two years earlier. I allowed myself to be transparent, and when I finished talking, former strangers came forward to love and accept me. It was an unexpected phenomenon. I had not dared to publicly reveal my emotions before, during or immediately after my battle with alcoholism—there was still the stigma, and I knew not what to expect—this was up close and personal—and all those people! The Holy Spirit came through for me and the words that God wanted to reach into the hearts of the listeners that day, flowed as if spoken by another. I felt an indescribable joy and warmth as I looked into the eyes of new friends who extended their hands to one whose life had been laid wide open and raw. One of the women who heard me speak had been having a problem with alcohol, and I began to meet with her. My sunroom on the lake was to become a haven for alcoholic women in search of understanding and hope.

Another church group invited me to speak and when finished, I was introduced to a staff member of the community hospital who suggested I work there out of the chaplaincy department or in some way try to connect with the alcohol patients. How interesting that there was a need in the one department I had stayed out of during my hospital volunteer work in California. I began my training as a volunteer lay-chaplain. I also enrolled in the humanities department at Marylhurst College in order to pick up some classes in psychology. I had taken some psych classes at California State in Fullerton and wanted to continue my learning in that field as well as in creative writing and communication. I developed a whole new love for school, and it was thrilling for me to learn and be able to comprehend. After so much abuse, my brain cells were multiplying, and with intensive studying, I found I was capable of a 4.0 GPA. Unlike my early school days when I wouldn't dare work hard to get good grades for fear I might stand out, combined with the home trauma that prevented me from concentrating on my studies, I began having the time of my life in the classroom. Marylhurst reminded me of FWP in Chicago from those many years ago—like a home with feelings in it—talented faculty who cared and whose teaching skills lasted, wood floors and radiators, high ceilings and sounds of music, climbing trees outside the old windows.

One of the communication classes at the college was taught by a visiting Portland State professor who agreed to let me do my oral term project on the disease of alcoholism, integrating my personal experiences. I spoke for almost an hour in front of seventeen hushed students and the professor, who said at the end of my talk, "Karen, you presented a fine talk on alcoholism, and you shared briefly your miraculous cure. What I don't understand is, why don't you give credit to yourself? God is out there someplace, but we have the power within ourselves to take care of our problems." She had not gotten the point. She was offering intellectual humanism. She granted me an additional ten minutes, during which time I gave my personal testimony. Two young women had come from alcoholic homes and they knew exactly what I was talking about, but they longed to know more about Christ. A leader of another church was in the class and invited me to speak to their youth group. One of the students asked for a show of hands to determine how many in our class were affected by alcoholism in their families. Two-thirds responded. A special bond developed in that classroom, and I've often wondered if the professor has since given more thought to the power of God and the personal relationship one can have with Jesus Christ.

My doctor in Oregon kept me on the same medications for a while, yet there were other patterns that were changing in my body as I tried desperately to stop smoking. The movie and television screen had shown me how to fashionably hold a cigarette. As socially sophisticated as the cocktail hour, smoking had long been acceptable. However, medical evidence linking cigarette smoking to cancer was on the rise, plus my own mother's death had personally illustrated another one of the dangers of smoking. Yet it was an addiction that assured me that I would smoke in spite of my best intentions.

We were sitting in front of the fire one evening in winter; Bill was reading, while I added a multitude of my photographs to our albums, smoking as I went along, wishing I were not so weak. Suddenly my chest began to burn as if on fire. I put out the cigarette, then lit another and tried to inhale. My throat burned, and I snuffed out the cigarette. I tried again, and to my utter amazement, I was unable to smoke. I hadn't said anything to Bill all the time this was going on—he might not believe me—I hardly believed it myself. I've not had a cigarette since then, nor has smoking been a part of my thought pattern since 1979.

To know God is to be fascinated by Him. I don't know why I hadn't asked to be healed of smoking. Surely I knew better than to underestimate the power of God. In retrospect, I was not accustomed to thinking of myself as so valuable to God that He would actually listen to my every prayer. To try to understand the depth of His caring and love for me was incomprehensible and to acknowledge my many weaknesses was something new in my life. Known by my family and friends to be a stubborn Norske, I was struggling to quit smoking by myself when it would have been so much easier to yield to God than to try to control in vain. Not only that, but as I came to realize, smoking was not the real issue. Knowing and loving God—giving myself to God with my heart and remembering that the rest will follow—that was the issue. God would take care of what I couldn't handle, and in my weakness, God again revealed Himself as the true strength of my life.

The business situation changed for the worse for Bill, and it was hard to tell David when he was home for Christmas that we were leaving the lake. Bill was in bed with the flu when Dave went with me to get our tree that we set up in the sunroom with a few lights and a star on top. The Austrian nativity was on the mantel nearby. Amid packing boxes we sat down for a candlelight Christmas dinner by the tree. Through the windows of our favorite room, the beauty of softly colored lights reflected upon the water from other homes around the lake, and we bowed our heads. David said the blessing, and he closed with "Please, dear Lord, help Mom to bear up under all this." It is a sweet thing to be bonded to a child by our faith.

$\mathcal{A}$ KNOWING BOND
23

Ten years after my hysterectomy, I was scheduled for another surgery when an abdominal mass was discovered. The evening before the operation, I read my Bible in the hospital room and came across Psalm 139. God's Word pulled me close to Him, and I knew in my heart that wherever I was, He would be—that He would take care of me regardless of whether I had terminal cancer, had to be sewn up immediately with just months to live—or if I died on the table. I knew I'd be with Him—or if He chose to give me a longer life on earth, I'd never be alone. The depth of comfort that I had assured me of His love. Not only a feeling but a fact. When I thought about my surgery ten years earlier when I was a difficult patient, controlled by alcoholism, fearful and uncertain, I thanked Him again for His peace. I was made so aware that He was my refuge and I was able to rest on that truth as prayer led me into His arms. Pastor Bob came to pray with me the following morning and held my hand as I was wheeled to surgery. His caring made a difference in my attitude as well. God chose to keep me healthy.

I remember lying down for a nap during my recuperation at home at a time when our daughter was having a biopsy for a possible melanoma. My forever friend Barb called and prayed for her over the phone, and afterward, I closed my eyes and felt a brush of air all around me in the room—like a slight ruffle of breeze. I lay there wondering if Bill had come home for lunch, but somehow I couldn't open my eyes to see—and then there was a most gentle kiss on my forehead. I opened my eyes and the air was still—no one was there. I asked Bill that night if he had been there, and he said no. There had been a presence in the room, and I've wondered ever since if it was the wings of an angel or my Lord.

I had some of the most significant years of my life as a volunteer lay-chaplain. We had six weeks of intensive training followed by monthly training sessions by the hospital chaplain. I also trained for a while in clinical pastoral education at Emanuel Hospital. One of "my" first patients was a woman who had suffered from alcoholism for many years. (We were taught to not refer to anyone we were working with as "my" patient—they "belonged to the Lord.")

"Jean" had no family and her friends had left her. "Have you ever been lonely?" she asked, staring at blue-gray sky from her hospital bed; "Do you have a tree in your yard?" I responded that yes, I had been lonely and had a tree. I held her hand when she spoke again, "When I get very lonely, I go out to my tree and put my arms around it. They don't reach of course, but it feels so good to hug."

Another patient said I was the first person who ever entered her hospital room and didn't look at her as though she were an "open sore." I hope I never forget how deeply the eyes of judgment can wound and the extent of unconditional love that must be ministered in its place.

One day, a young mother was brought into intensive care. Alcoholism had caused her heart to stop several times, and her kidneys had stopped functioning. She was lapsing into a coma. I later wrote this about my Finnish friend:

The Brief Gift
I didn't know you when you were well,
When fully alive and real.
They wheeled you in to intensive care,
A young blond mother of two . . .
And I stayed by your side.
We could have been friends, I thought . . .
There was a knowing bond.

Your skin so fair, your breathing faint,
Large hazel eyes that betray you.
The fear and the plea from silent lips
To shut off your life. I couldn't of course,
But felt your pain.

There was no hope, and how long
Your family wondered . . . would you be dead
To them and remain alive?
And I put my arms around them and they left . . .
Too much to bear.

I held your hand, bowed my head and prayed . . .
Your fears were over, your trembling gone.
A "still" awareness when He reached down
To lift the you
Up in His arms . . . unspoken peace.

We'll meet again, dear friend. You broke
Their hearts, they didn't understand . . .
That's why God let me be with you at
The end.

$\mathcal{N}$OT AN ILLNESS TO JUDGE . . . NOR A SIN TO DENY

24

$\mathcal{A}$ lcoholism is a diagnosis . . . not an accusation . . . the stigma is in not doing something about it!"[5] Alcoholics are not members of the hall of failure—the so-called average alcoholic is a man or woman with family, job and responsibilities. I was able to function quite well for most of my years of addiction. Though driven, I nevertheless accomplished a great deal of good for the benefit of our community. The alcoholic doesn't have control over the brain biochemistry—he or she is different—they're sick. A capsulized description of alcoholism is ". . . a chronic, progressive, incurable disease characterized by loss of control over alcohol and other sedatives."[6]

Alcoholism became identified as a legitimate disease in 1956. The most commonly used drug in the world, alcohol's the only drug that can be classified as a food. It has calories and very little in the way of vitamins and minerals. The alcoholic is taking in so many calories from the alcohol that he or she will require or even want fewer calories from nutritional foods, resulting in malnutrition. The alcohol impairs the absorption of nutrients in the intestine, also causing malnutrition and deficiency of vitamin B1, resulting in neurological damage to the brain.

Sin belongs to the grocery store chains whose liquor departments are larger than the produce or dairy sections.

Response of the alcoholic in recovery or attempting to be—"Please don't tempt me—please don't make me walk past the wine to get the milk—this isn't fair—please help me—I want to be responsible, but I need your understanding and cooperation. Please be fair."

Sin belongs to the cottage industry who labels their gourmet packages of soup beans with recipe comments like, "Just wait, we're getting to the wine next!" and, "Refill your own wine glass if necessary," and, "Pour wine in glass and slowly sip as you proceed with directions."

Response of the alcoholic in recovery or attempting to be—"I don't have wine in the house anymore, and I won't buy your products ever again—I just wanted to make some good bean soup, not be tempted by wine or read a recipe that encourages it."

Sin belongs to the man who says his "wife can't be an alcoholic because she's a Christian," to the woman who says her "daughter-in-law can't be an alcoholic because of her faith."

Response of the alcoholic in recovery or attempting to be—"Please! Try to understand! It has nothing to do with being a Christian. If you have a faith, don't judge me—help me to get well. There but by the grace of God go you or any one of us."

Sin belongs to the pastor who says from the pulpit, "We (in terms of we who are *right* in such matters—the pastoral staff) are not addressing the alcoholic, the bum, we're addressing the Christian," *and* to the minister who preaches, "You can be an alcoholic if you're dumb enough to be one."

Response of the alcoholic in recovery or attempting to be—"Are you talking to me? Do you know about me? Does anyone know? I've got to get out of here! I came here to be lifted up, not slapped down. Please don't hate me! Please don't think I'm a bum. *And* you're my pastor! Please don't judge! I didn't choose to be this way, and I'm trying to change. I thought I was in a place where there would be caring and unconditional love. And you're accusing me! I hope I can help you to understand when I feel stronger."

A person can become a chronic alcoholic without showing the symptoms of drunkenness. At every stage, the disease itself can prevent the alcoholic from realizing he or she is addicted to alcohol. During middle and late stages, the alcoholic cannot see themselves as others see them. Research tells us that the brain suffers from various degrees of chemical toxicity; therefore, there is memory impairment. The addicted individual is unable to see the truth and cannot accept, therefore, cannot be motivated to deal with something that he or she denies. To quote Anderson Spickard, Jr., a professor of medicine at Vanderbilt University Medical Center, "To tell an alcoholic to shape up and stop drinking is like telling a man who has just jumped out a nine-story building to fall only three floors. It just isn't going to happen."

We didn't know that I was a predisposed genetically inherent alcoholic—we didn't realize that the disease begins long before one begins to act or think like an alcoholic, not even conscious of the changes that are taking place in the body. The alcoholic is not responsible for those initial changes. The prime time for the disease to take hold is when a woman is in her twenties and early thirties. I was thirty-one when my mother died—her death seemed to trigger something in my own system to be turned upside down—the trauma seemed to cause an inner chemical pandemonium that could not be explained or accepted.

Sin belongs to the one who says alcoholics are bad people who need to be good and repent or else.

Response of the alcoholic in recovery or attempting to be—"I feel like a drowning cripple who is left to struggle for survival alone. *And* I don't want to be bad—inside I'm really good—I'm sorry I disappoint you, too—I'm sorry, I'm sorry, I'm sorry."

The brain, liver, heart, pancreas, lungs, kidney and every other organ and tissue system are infiltrated by alcohol within minutes after it pours into the blood stream. Nothing can be done to hurry the process of metabolism. Alcohol changes the metabolism of some heart cells causing uncontrolled fluttering—fibrillation—of the heart, possible heart attack as well as arrhythmias—disturbances in the heart's rhythm. And alcohol can cause birth defects.[7]

Sin belongs to the media that shows virtually all one-hour dramas with people drinking, which is TV's heavy drinking problem, according to Dr. James DeFoe, renowned expert in the field of alcoholism.

Sin belongs to the joker at the office Christmas party who spikes the alternate nonalcoholic punch and to the mindless dad or mom who provides beer for the high school kegger.

Sin belongs to parents and teenagers who refuse to take the time to be educated about alcohol and the multiple addiction of alcohol and drugs.

Response of the alcoholic in recovery or attempting to be—"Can't you enact a scene without a drink in your hand? Why do you make it look so good? So acceptable? So necessary in order to be social?"

And "I really tried to please everyone at this party! There's an alcoholic punch and a nonalcoholic punch. I forgive you because you just don't understand, but I'm sorry you think it's funny and okay to spike the punch. Not everyone here can handle it. Can you?"

An alcoholic loses control because the body's tolerance steadily decreases and the withdrawal symptoms increase. One of the worst effects of alcohol is directly on the brain. Psychosis, confusion or unconsciousness can result. Maintenance drinking is to keep the balance level, which is a protective device within the alcoholic. For some people, the body's adaptation to alcohol occurs within weeks or months—in others, years can go by before the person's addiction is obvious, at which point he or she becomes a victim of an insidious, progressive and often fatal disease they have no control over.

Sin belongs to the church that casts its people out who have problems with alcohol, drugs and/or cigarettes. The individual is so frowned upon that he or she feels unworthy to go anywhere near church, including for counseling, and is no longer contacted by the heads of that church. And yet he or she is powerless to change without help.

Response of the alcoholic in recovery or attempting to be—"I feel so alone. I need my church family—please don't reject me. I don't know where else to turn. Shouldn't there be love and help here?"

In 1983 (unfortunately very little has changed since then) Professor Spickard responded to the question of whether or not churches are responding adequately to the presence of alcoholics in its midst and in society at large.

> The church should be in the forefront of efforts to help alcoholics because alcoholism has a pronounced spiritual dimension. Unfortunately, the church reflects the attitudes of society as a whole and looks at alcoholics as weak-willed and hopeless. Even well-meaning

Christians tend to beat alcoholics over the head with a Bible, warning them to repent of their sin, and telling them not to come back to church until they can stop drinking. The alcoholic, no matter how sorry he feels, cannot stop—and he won't be back.

Many church members successfully conceal their alcoholism for years. They go to their pastors complaining of family or personal problems, but the root of their problem is never recognized and confronted. As their alcoholism progresses, these people drop out of church altogether. They can no longer afford the mental anguish that comes from rubbing shoulders with people they perceive as evangelical. The Christian alcoholic becomes convinced that he has lost his salvation, and he doesn't darken the door of a church again. In this way he is effectively cut off from the people who should be (among the) most qualified to help him.

It's a myth that when the alcoholic is drinking, he or she reveals his or her true personality. I was so relieved to discover this truth! The reality is that the alcohol's effect on the brain causes severe psychological and emotional distortions of the normal personality. Sobriety is what reveals the true personality of the alcoholic.

Alcoholics often die before their disease is diagnosed, and heart failure is a major cause of death. In early, mid to late stages of the disease, an alcoholic can go through the DTs, and the condition is so stressful that any other medical problem occurring simultaneously, such as pancreatitis or liver disease, heart or gastrointestinal disease can cause fatal breakdown in the alcoholic's already seriously over-stressed body. Sometimes the trauma alone of the DTs can precipitate a massive coronary, brain hemorrhage or respiratory shutdown. The mortality rate of an alcoholic suffering DTs is forty times higher than that of a heroin addict going through withdrawals. DTs would kill more alcoholics if accidents, suicides and other diseases didn't kill them first.[6]

Sin belongs to the man who tells his wife that there's something appealing about her helplessness. Since when does the male ego have to be nourished by needless suffering?

Sin belongs to the man who beats his alcoholic wife for drinking.

Sin belongs to the physician who prescribes wine for relaxation or diversion to the young, overworked, stressed mom or to the widowed alcoholic heart patient who doesn't have long to live anyway.

Alcohol impairs the immune system; it enlarges the red blood cells causing high blood pressure; the tingling of fingers and toes indicates that the nerves are gradually losing their ability to transmit sensory and motor signals; alcohol alters the hormone balance so the body is in permanent distress. It disrupts the menstrual cycle. It upsets the blood sugar balance causing damage to the pancreas. In an alcoholic, the liver cells have been likened to an eerie battlefield. It is a possible contributor to cancer. Pneumonia is a common complication, and its death rate is seven times higher for women than the general population.

A quote from Dr. David Olhms says it like it is. "To those who still say it's a matter of willpower, all I can say is that the less one knows about an illness, the more likely one is to have stereotyped beliefs about it, and the main problem with stereotypes is that they're often incorrect."[6]

Sin belongs to the man who says he can't afford medical treatment for his wife although it would be different if she had breast cancer, heart disease or arthritis.

Sin belongs to the priest and minister who serve wine during communion.

Sin belongs to the dad who will tell his daughter about his vasectomy but won't talk to her about her mother's alcohol induced insanity.

Sin belongs to the husband who sexually abuses his alcoholic wife because she's out of it anyway!

An alcoholic abusing only alcohol is very rare. The majority of alcoholics have a multiple addiction, and too many die combining Valium and other tranquilizers and antidepressants with their drinking. Alcohol and prescription drugs equal a chemical time bomb. One drink and one pill can multiply the potency three to four times. There are several tranquilizers and antidepressants that are considered dangerous to the alcoholic as well as to the recovering alcoholic. Women seem to be the scapegoats for multiple addiction problems. As long as the alcoholic drinks, her health issues will get worse, so she is then given prescriptions for depression, anemia, palpitations, colitis etc. Because of cross-tolerance, she will increase the dosage to get the desired effect with possible fatal complications.

Sin belongs to the psychologist, psychiatrist, doctor, all who prescribe medications to the admitted, suspected or recovering alcoholic that are as dangerous as the alcohol itself, if not more so. "Cross-tolerance can result in coma, convulsions, respiratory failure and death."[8]

Sin belongs to the physician who orders a morphine machine for an alcoholic to use for pain after a routine major surgery.

Blackouts are experienced in the alcoholic but not in the nonalcoholic! The events that happen are not just forgotten, they are not even stored in the brain. So there's nothing to be recalled later. These blackouts can occur in early stages but definitely in mid and later stages. During this time, the alcoholic will be aware of what's going on around him or her and can eat, walk, drive a car, conduct business, make promises but later has no memory trace of it whatsoever. The amount of time lost can be minutes, hours or days.

"Wet brain" is a term used when enough alcohol is consumed to cause unconsciousness, dangerously near the amount needed to paralyze the respiratory center, shut off the breathing apparatus and kill the alcoholic. Wet brain is usually irreversible—one in thirty-six have a chance to recover.

Sin belongs to the spouse who says, "I just pay the bills."

Sin belongs to the informed and educated alcoholic physician who refuses treatment for himself and/or his wife. Doctors, above all others, should deal honestly and wisely with the disease.

Sin belongs to the informed and educated adult child of an alcoholic who makes the conscious choice to drink because "it won't happen to me."

As Betty Ford says, "It is an equal opportunity disease." With effective intervention and treatment, even the most advanced alcoholic has a chance to get well. No intervention is a failure! Even if the alcoholic refuses treatment, the family becomes stronger, and it could save one of their lives in the future. Remember—84 percent will recover if given treatment at any stage. A process pioneered by The Johnson Institute in Minnesota, "intervention" with dignity is one of the kindest things one can do for an alcoholic in an atmosphere of love and caring. Without an intervention, thoughts of the alcoholic may include, "Don't you care enough to confront? Don't you care about my life? Please love me enough. I can't do this by myself. I feel so helpless. Please." Hopefully the alcoholic is sober when a gathering takes place, but there is usually no such thing as a perfect time. Family, pastor, boss, doctor or friends surrounding her or him relate situations during which they were deeply hurt or offended or frightened by the behavior of the addicted person. The alcoholic may refuse to believe it at all or may give in and be willing to accept treatment because of those who love her or him. After the intervention, it is up to the individual alcoholic.

Sin belongs to the spouse who chooses to be in denial rather than change his own lifestyle.

Sin belongs to the alcoholic who refuses to take responsibility for treatment offered during a fair intervention.

One of the most confusing aspects of the disease is that the alcoholic feels most ill, not when he or she drinks, but when they stop drinking, which can be for days, weeks or months. Seizures are common during withdrawal. Dr. E.M. Jelinek (1890-1963), who conducted his research at Yale University and was the first to define medically and to chart the progression of the disease into its various stages, said that "the abstinent alcoholic will continue to suffer from protracted withdrawal symptoms until the healing process is complete—sometimes for years. The cells are still suffering from damage caused by the alcohol and need time to recover. Depression, anxiety, insomnia, fears, conscious or unconscious thoughts of feeling weak and psychologically sick affect the majority of (recovering) alcoholics. Without nutritional therapy, they may never fully recover."

Dr. David Olhms is a pioneer in the field of alcoholism and is a psychiatrist. He began to study, help and treat the disease because he discovered that psychiatry doesn't help the alcoholic. He says, "Alcoholism is not primarily a psychological disease, and once the psychiatrists grasp the fact that alcoholism is primarily a physiologically based disease, their role will change dramatically, and they can learn to treat the alcoholic. They will be able to get their patients into recovery instead of attempting to treat the mind."

Though controversial, Dr. Olhms believes it a fact that the alcoholic has a substance in their brain tissue that's closely related to heroin—actually a breakdown product of heroin. Contrary to the nonalcoholic, when the alcoholic drinks, the alcohol is diverted and becomes THIQ—long identified as Tetro Hydro Iso Quinala—and the control is gone.

The Wellness Letter, published by the University of California at Berkeley has come up with some interesting geographical findings, Such as, of over one hundred million people in the United States, ten million are alcoholics, and 25 to 50 percent of these are women. Great Britain ranks first and the Soviet Union second. I think it's interesting that Jews and Italians, who have had access to large amounts of alcohol for over seven thousand years, have a very low rate of alcoholism. Northern European countries, including France, Ireland and the Scandinavian countries, have had access to alcohol for fifteen hundred years, and the rate of alcoholism is relatively high. Native Americans didn't have alcohol until about three hundred years ago and suffer from an extremely high rate of alcoholism. Recent studies conducted in Japan have shown that 50 percent of all Orientals do not produce the liver enzyme that metabolizes alcohol; therefore, those individuals cannot drink at all without becoming obviously ill.

Medical science says that "children who are raised in alcoholic homes are more apt to become alcoholics; however, studies have shown that a significant number of children born of alcoholic parents, when raised in a nonalcoholic home, still do become alcoholics." The genetic predisposition to alcoholism practically guarantees that the child of one alcoholic parent has a 50 to 60 percent chance of becoming an alcoholic while the child of two alcoholic parents bears a 75 to 80 percent chance!

Church intercession is possible. Dr. Spickard, who conducts church seminars, shares that "the church must have a core of people who have educated themselves in the areas of chemical dependency and alcoholism. There are many helpful books available, and it is possible for anyone to become quite knowledgeable in only a short period of time." According to Dr. Spickard, "In two hours they will know more about alcoholism than 90 percent of all physicians. This core group can then educate the rest of the church. Not every church needs to have its own counseling service, but someone in the church needs to know where to find the nearest professional help."

Sin belongs to us all! We need to be willing to raise our level of awareness and compassion. We need to be educated. Our schools and churches, corporations and governments should be strong areas for teaching and guiding. There have been some good beginnings. Strength comes in numbers, however, and we need a national, even international enlightenment.

The disease of alcoholism is not a choice!

BALANCE, PLEASE
25

*T*he more I know, the more amazed I am at the astonishing miracle that God chose to provide for me. I didn't know how ill I was; I didn't know about the complications of alcoholism; I didn't know about cross-tolerance; I didn't have an understanding of what a multiple addiction is; I was never treated for alcoholism, only for some of the results and complications of the disease, and that almost killed me. An unthinking person will find it easy to walk through danger; I feel like I spent twelve and a half years of my life with a frozen conscience, without the ability to grasp reality, an alien hiding in my own shadow.

Christ provided me with His divine intervention. He changed *me* when He healed me of alcoholism. As Dr. Norman Vincent Peale wrote to me a year ago, "You have been set free. Freedom from everything that limits life. You have been given freedom in its highest form by the grace and love of God." Can there be anything more exciting?

The light of Christ broke the patterns that had been so long-standing in my mother's life, in the generations before her, and in mine—the diseased, man-made patterns that destroy life. My helplessness and secret shame were replaced with courage and a healthy perseverance. I was so thrilled to be free of alcohol that I was able to be very up-front with my doctors and immediately made it known that I had been an alcoholic. Yet I was continuing to have fears of driving, insomnia, headaches, the frequent feeling that I didn't have my equilibrium, palpitations—they were all puzzling to me. Why couldn't my informed and educated doctor make me feel more in-balance? When in anxious situations—simple, routine activities as driving on the freeway or trying to hold a cup of coffee while walking across a room—I began to practice the presence of Christ in my every day living. The prayer I kept with me in the car really helped:

> *The Light of God surrounds me.*
> *The Love of God enfolds me.*
> *The Power of God protects me.*
> *The Presence of God watches over me.*
> *Wherever I am, God is.*
>
> *Author unknown*

I trained myself to take deep breaths—Jesus breaths as I called them—and they worked!

I was taking Premarin and Synthroid, was taken off Placydil and given Dalmane for sleep. Elavil was prescribed and finally Adapin for an antidepressant. Lasix was added, and I continued to take Librax for my colon. My body had taken so much abuse, it didn't occur to me that I was still suffering the withdrawal symptoms of the multiple addiction. So when my doctor sent me to a psychologist to help me with the insomnia and fears and anxieties, I figured my mind must really be out of whack, and that's the way I guessed I'd always be. At the same time, I was able to think clearly and be a responsible person. I was loving my hospital work and enjoying a 4.0 GPA in my classes at a nearby college—yet what did I know about body chemistry?

Listen to me, Doctor, please
1985

The psychologist tried hypnosis for the insomnia and after trying to cooperate, I finally burst out laughing. I felt badly for him that I couldn't be hypnotized, but it just wasn't working. He then suggested that we go out on the freeway—that I'd be fine and safe because he was with me. He didn't understand that I felt safest on the roads when by myself and not responsible for a passenger. The issue of my medications was never discussed, and I left with the same complaints I had when I began with him, and with the same prescriptions.

I was still anemic and short of breath, and I began having stomach spasms. I also felt something I can only describe as an ongoing electrical current vibrating inside of me from head to toe. The doctor termed them "seizures" when he changed me from Dalmane to Halcyon. In response to my complaint, he also told me I looked too good to feel like I was in a pressure cooker. At the same time he told me how out of whack my body chemistry was, and I needed to get a handle on my fears. I had worked so hard—what was happening that I sensed confusion and fears attempting to grab me? Disillusionment was invading me. Additional symptoms that I told him about included blurred vision, heaviness in my chest, metal taste and parched lips, nausea, feeling of fullness in my ears, unsteady legs. And then, when he decided that I may still be experiencing withdrawal symptoms from Dalmane and he began to wean me from Halcyon, I realized that I didn't have to accept the unacceptable. While the doctor had been trying new medications on me, he was simultaneously adjusting the dosages of my other medications including the hormone and thyroid prescriptions. I had begun to learn how to focus on God and seek His wisdom through prayer, to share prayer concerns with close friends, and to trust the Holy Spirit for His direction. I decided to change physicians and made several calls to the main hospitals and to friends for references. It's imperative for the woman with an addictive body chemistry to get medical care from a physician who really knows how to treat the chemical imbalance. We have to be willing to search for that doctor and not settle for anything less. When our self-esteem has been in the gutter of life for any period of time, it's easy to think we're not worth quite so much trouble.

To be told, first by an endocrinologist, then an internist who became my primary physician, that I was over medicated was like music to my ears. My complexities were controllable after all! It wasn't my mind—the reasons for the way I was feeling were *valid*! I could compare it to the relief of discovering that my true personality was revealed not when I was under the influence of alcohol, but when completely sober—cleansed and free of the poison. Theories, medical and scientific facts about alcoholism and multiple addictions may change, and I don't know if the controversy will ever be settled. What I *do* know is that my own body chemistry is different—that what alcohol does to me, it doesn't do to everyone. People can call it anything they want—in my system, it's a parasite. It's what happened to *me* that I have to tell. Genetics, environment, chemistry all have a part in the puzzle.

Researcher John Crabbe says, "You inherit genes; you don't inherit alcoholism, and the genes control some specific trait." What alcoholism researchers don't know is how many genes are involved and exactly what it is people inherit that predisposes them to alcoholism. Crabbe, like Dr. Olhms, works with mice and also finds that "one of the things that alcohol does in very low doses is destroy their sense of balance." Also, Crabbe's withdrawing seizure-prone mice have "shown more of a marked withdrawal from diazepan—Valium—and barbiturates than his withdrawal-resistant mice, which suggests that a predisposition to alcoholism may also predispose to these other drugs of dependence."[9]

I'm finding that I can sometimes sleep without a pill, and that's a statement I never thought I'd be able to make. My driving is finally free of apprehension, and I zip around on the freeways, short or long distances, without anxieties. Palpitations and headaches are gone. I can carry a cup of coffee across an empty or crowded room, and I can walk on a marbleized floor without feeling that I'm losing my balance. Taking an escalator is fairly easy, and my hand tremors are completely gone. I don't experience mood swings or nausea or feelings of suspension. I'm on the lowest dose of Premarin and Synthroid and temporarily on twenty milligrams of the antidepressant Prozac. Though controversial, for me Prozac is very effective, and I'm being carefully monitored. I feel balanced! And what is exciting to me is that as my doctor is weaning me off of Prozac, to where I am taking one twenty-milligram dose every three days now, I continue to feel balanced. To me, that is somewhat of another miracle. It will soon be the first time in thirty years that I will be completely free of an antidepressant or tranquilizer!

I began a Bible study in my home for Women In Need—of help and spiritual support to overcome the disease of alcoholism and prescription drug addiction. Called **W+n** with a Cross," the women are potential *winners*, and we laugh as much as we weep for one another as we read and try to absorb God's Word together; we also use Claire W.'s workbook titled, *God, Help Me Stop!* We experience a freedom to express our thoughts that wouldn't feel safe elsewhere. There's a commitment of real caring, encouragement for medical treatment, if needed, and additional support groups.

In our way of thinking, as *winners*, the liberated woman is not a feminist; she is a woman who is free of the polluted stigma of alcoholism and is loved, valued and accepted in spite of her misunderstood disease. We also know better than to strive for the "supermom—perfect home" image and mentality. I am free of all those burdens of guilt and troublesome self-demands because of the peace of Christ. Medical science will never completely understand the complexities of our body chemistry. Only our Creator knows the total being.

I'd love to know how to give a crash course in sober adulthood! *Winners* feel we've missed a lot, and it's a humbling revelation that God chose each one of us to be the mother of the children we have, the wife to our husband, and friend to our friends, His knowing all along the way what grief would be brought to them. So why me? As Frankie, one of my Christian role models, would say, "Why not me?" When I ran away to Solvang, thinking *anyone* could be a better wife, mother or friend, that was never the point. God had made His choice long ago, and I would not have missed my miracle for anything.

It is not enough to be committed to home and family. To be a complete woman is to be committed to Christ. For the benefit of my husband and children and the healthy, traditional values I yearned to know and provide in our home, it would have been most enlightening and reassuring had I known to listen to someone like today's Dr. James Dobson's Focus on the Family and Charles Swindoll's Insight for Living radio ministries. Probably because of abandonment by my biological father and a distant, sometimes fearful relationship with my adoptive dad, it took me a few years to be able to say "Father" in my prayers. The Bible tells us that the Lord "restores for you the years the locusts have eaten," (Joel 2:25), and that is another wonderful truth I can share. When looking through the eyes of faith and placing Christ first in her life, a woman can see things differently and she doesn't need to wear a mask. As trust and faith build, she learns to allow her daily habitual weaknesses to lead her to Him, and she can believe in twentieth century miracles.

TRUSTING HEARTS
26

There were other areas of interest in my hospital ministry. I studied medical ethics during Clinical Pastoral Education training and served on an ethics committee. Terminal cancer patients struggle with pain, hopelessness, frightening deterioration of the body, the inability to share feelings with those closest to them, and sometimes the denial of a husband who refuses to believe this is happening and often leaves the scene. I learned to help the patient talk about the life that had been lived and the death that would end it. God used me to write and to give eulogies. It has been a revelation to me that we as Christians are qualified, as well as called, to minister to others in such ways.

I worked in labor and delivery and the neonatal care unit. One day I was asked by our instructor what I'd do if I were asked to baptize an infant. Unless my personal faith conflicted, which it did not, he convinced me that God uses all of us to minister to the needs of people where they are at the time. About six weeks later, I was called into the emergency room at another hospital where a four-month-old baby girl was being brought in as a SIDS case—Sudden Infant Death Syndrome. I had seen other SIDS babies and witnessed the incredible pain that sweeps through the staff members as the most valiant effort is made to revive a child whose life has probably already been claimed. I guided the

mother into the trauma room to say goodbye to one of the most beautiful babies I had ever seen—her head capped with soft brown curls—"Jennie's" perfectly formed, stone-gray body now lay free of most tubes and instruments. We sat next to the gurney in a room so opposed to the warmth of a nursery, while her mom rocked her gently in her arms and tears had to be held by the hand of God. The mom spoke quietly, "We were going to have her baptized in a few weeks," to which I responded that I could baptize Jennie right here if she'd like, and she nodded her head. I asked for a small dish of sterile water, remembering recent instructions. She asked where her baby was right now, and I shared simply my belief that the Bible says all little children go into the kingdom of God when they die. This was for Jennie's mother, who continued to hold her ever so tenderly, as I baptized her baby. Mom was ready to leave then, and as we stood up together, she handed Jennie to me. I held her close as her mother left the room and silently expressed my humble gratitude to God for the unexpected opportunity and the trust that had been placed in me because of Him. The heaviness of the body surprised me, yet the light of her life had been lifted and the essence of Jennie had gone to be with Christ Jesus. It was a strange phenomenon—the railings of the gurney were down as I placed her on top of the white sheet; a mother doesn't leave a child alone with the crib railings down—but I could trust Him.

While I was writing in my journal in the chaplaincy office, an island of memories caught my attention, and I thought of the helplessness of the four-month-old baby girl at Children's Hospital in California many years earlier. Where I had then struggled with the responsibility of holding a fragile life, there was no apprehension here. Different circumstances didn't make the difference. By the grace of God, I very simply am not what I was. Inner peace and assurance have come to replace sorrow and fear because of the presence of God in my life.

"7-4-7-4"—*emergency*—came over the intercom. It was time to help with another patient. "Mary" had overdosed on drugs and alcohol. When asked how many pills she had taken, she said, "I don't know—every time I wake up, I take a few." I remembered those nights of my own as I listened to Mary talk about being so alone and afraid that if screaming in her closet didn't help, she'd get into her car and drive around the lake with windows rolled up so that people couldn't hear her screams. If her fear of losing touch with her feelings continued, then Mary knew no other way but to drink and take prescribed sedatives.

A cancer patient who was deeply depressed over his wife's recent death was brought into emergency and "Tom" told me later that his wife had suffered from alcoholism and died from the complications of pancreatitis and hepatitis. Because of her admitted alcoholism, an unforgivable sin in their church, the bishop and elders told this couple that they would not offer prayer and would not be supportive during her dying days—therefore, a Catholic priest gave her last rites at her hospital bedside. Tom promised his "word of mouth would do them harm."

Forty-three year old "Sue" was admitted to intensive care. As a result of years of chronic alcoholism, she would not recover this time. She had become so desperate, that she had ordered a case of Scope mouthwash and a case of hair spray to supplement her liquor supply. She ended up in a coma and attached to machines. I prayed aloud that her heart would yield to the love of God. In my years of drinking, it had never occurred to me to obtain alcohol from anything but liquor. (Scope mouthwash is 18.9 percent alcohol, and Listerine is 26.9 percent alcohol.) Ultimately, Sue became a non-functioning "vegetable," and lived the rest of her life in a foster home. Another patient had abused her body by drinking hair spray, vanilla extract and cough syrups.

"Lynn" said she was so ashamed of "failing God and being a society defect" that she didn't want to wake up again. She had gone to a new doctor, had given him her complete history including the alcoholism. He prescribed Xanax, a lethal tranquilizer when consumed with alcohol.

One of my friends said that she didn't know any alcoholics and, surely, none were in her neighborhood. I visited "Carol," who was back in the hospital as a result of alcohol and Valium addiction that had been her private shame all during the years she was taking care of my friend's children in her own home down the neighborhood street. Carol expressed her view that "the world looked dirty when [she] got sober." In other words, there was no unconditional love, there was no hope, only shame and disgust and moral judgment toward her from society. "Mary" told me that if she ever got to heaven it would be on "eggshells" because of the "sin" in her life. How can one repent from disease? Alcohol abuse—drunkenness—is a sin. Disease is not a sin!

The pattern in alcoholics reveals that they are hardest on themselves. Even in recovery, a woman's emotional war continues to fight the forgiveness of herself. The ugliness of the disease claws at self-respect and our potential is difficult to realize or acknowledge. With unsolicited scars from multiple addiction, it's difficult to comprehend that what nourishes the spirit isn't selfish, it's essential. And scars allow those of us in support groups to relate to one another while trusting hearts find their places in understanding and acceptance.

We're taught in chaplaincy training that we are not there to attack patients with Christianity—rather to meet them where they're at, to be a visitor and, hopefully, let Christ be reflected in our attitude and actions. It's been interesting to me to learn how many so-called atheists who are dying of cancer or alcoholism or heart disease cry out to God in the end—not to Joe or Ellen or the door knob—but to the Lord they need and want to reach.

Because of who he is and whom he represents, one of the highlights in my life was to be involved in the 1992 Billy Graham Crusade in Portland and see him face to face. His simple message of Jesus Christ being the answer—the way, the truth and the light—is true. It's a matter of relationship. It's a matter of a yielding and trusting heart.

B Y His Grace

27

On our way home to Oregon after a visit to southern California in May of '88, Bill and I stopped in Solvang for part of a day. It was the first time I had been back, and it was hard for me to understand the uncertain feelings inside of me. The Meadowlark Motel was still there, the same churches on either side, and I got out of the car to take a picture. I loved seeing the old gnarled tree still standing in front, and I had a fleeting desire to see Room 12. On this clear day, I wanted to walk across the field of blue lupine to the glen of the rainbow even though I knew it would be different. Too early for dinner, we drove back into town and walked the shops. Nothing interested me—a waste of time. I had no expectations, yet I wished I could get a grasp on what I was feeling and just why I was experiencing this vague uneasiness. To lie down on the warmth of the green grass under a tree somewhere appealed to the yearning within to try to absorb and understand what was happening inside of me. I had met the Lord here—nothing else mattered.

Dinnertime snapped me back as we opened the door to the Molenkroen Restaurant. At the top of the stairs, our table was near the post in the same room where I had been seated fourteen years earlier. But the atmosphere was dulled and very plain by comparison. Following a delicious meal, the after-dinner liqueur was served, and I spoke a silent prayer of thanks as I easily passed my glass to Bill. Christ, and all that is truth, had come into my heart—never again to be outside of me.

As we began to drive out of Solvang, the gentle golden hills darkening in the evening twilight, my heart welled up with tears, and I couldn't explain why I was suddenly over-whelmed with emotion and unable to talk. Then it came to me. I was weeping for the person who had died there—the Karen, who once was lost—it had been like revisiting an old grave and there was a figure to be mourned.

As the old had been buried back there in darkness, so was the pattern of my alcoholism destroyed. The passion that now filled my heart was for my Lord in humble grati-tude for His mercy and His grace upon me. I thought about 2 Corinthians 5:17, "Therefore, if anyone is in Christ, he is a new creature; the old is gone, the new has come." The Lord had met me right where I was, and had created a new creature—a new life—free to live with joy in the light of truth and hope—free to be a woman with love in my soul and allegiance to Jesus Christ—free to share my gift of faith that began with faith as small as a grain of mustard seed in a little motel room.

I would never have to wonder, "Where will I go when I die?" When Christ changed me, He changed my destiny. We see most clearly when we have an enlightened heart, and I left the tears of sadness behind.

My grace is sufficient for you, for my power is made perfect in weakness. 2 Corinthians 12:9

*H*OPE HAS A FUTURE
28

I was telling all of this to my forever friend Barbara as we continued to drive the winding road far beyond Peterborough, New Hampshire, as twilight beckoned the end of our October day of nostalgia four years ago. "Why didn't you tell me about the pain you were having all those years?" she asked. I shared with her that it wasn't until God healed me of alcoholism that the hurting memories began to heal. I was then given the freedom and confidence to *tell* and to *feel* and to *trust*. He gave me the courage to speak openly and to address the issue particularly with other women who are paying too high a price in life. He gave me complete trust in Him and He gave me the rainbow—God's promise of grace and mercy—an everlasting covenant He wants to share with us all.

"I wish I had your faith!" she exclaimed.

"I couldn't have my faith without my journey through the valley of brokenness. The whole pattern was hand-tailored for me," I responded. Hope has a future—hope has dreams in it.

We buttoned our woolen sweaters and turned on the car heater as autumn darkness fell over the Monadnock Mountains of New Hampshire. And I thought I saw the light of the beacon making its familiar pattern through the sky—not limited to guiding the way from atop Chicago's Palmolive Building a thousand miles to the west—the light of the beacon signified Christ to me now—the limitless light of the world as He shines over our lives. Christ, the beacon light that found me as a helpless child and led me to Him. No longer lost, but found. My heart would be in love with that light forever, and as we drove the darkening road along shadows of fir trees and birch, we followed the light of the one who shows us the way.

THE ⁻ᵢ⁻ END

APPENDIX ONE
MY PRESCRIBED DRUGS AND INTERACTION WITH ALCOHOL

Drug Names	Prescribed For	Overdose Effect	With Alcohol
*Elavil *Triavil	Depression	**Hallucinations, insomnia, coma	Stroke, warning to not combine, lethal
*Thorazene *Stelazine	Tranquilizer	Convulsions, coma	Jaundice, dangerous over-sedation
*Lomotyl	Intestinal cramps, diarrhea	Rapid heartbeat, coma	Jaundice, depressed brain function
Orinase	Diabetes, mellitus	Jaundice	Interferes with effectiveness of Rx, rapid pulse

Drug Names	Prescribed For	Overdose Effect	With Alcohol
*Librium	Tranquilizer, muscle spasms	Affects part of brain that controls emotions, coma, hallucinations	Potentially lethal, should be considered similar to alcohol and barbiturates
*Placydil	Hypnotic sleep inducer	Hallucinations, seizures, stomach pain, deep coma	Warning—dangerous excessive depressant
*Valium	Tranquilizer	Breathing difficulty, jaundice, deep coma	Warning—dangerous ***delirium, death
varieties of the Pill	Birth control	Drowsiness	No proven problems, do not take if liver dysfunction
Viokase	Replaces pancreatic enzyme deficiency	Irregular, rapid heartbeat	Unknown

My Prescribed Drugs and Interaction with Alcohol

Drug Names	Prescribed For	Overdose Effect	With Alcohol
Tincture of Bella Donna	Spasms of digestive system	Hallucinations, coma, convulsions, delirium common	Dangerous
Librax	Reduce spasms	Rapid heartbeat	Increased sedation, coma

*   Habit forming.

**   Hallucinations are a profound disorder in the central nervous system.

***   Delirium is a temporary mental disturbance characterized by hallucinations, agitation and incoherence.

APPENDIX TWO
DRUGS ALCOHOLICS SHOULD AVOID[10]

A partial list of drugs demonstrated to be dangerous to active alcoholics

All sedatives such as: Nembutal, Seconal, Tuinal, Quaalude, Dalmane, Placydil.
All narcotics such as: Codeine, Morphine, Heroin, Demerol.
All tranquilizers, and of special danger are: Valium and Librium.
Most pain-relieving medications including: Darvon and Talwin.
All antihistamines.
Drugstore medications containing antihistamines or scopolamine: Nytol, Sominex, Dristan.
Almost all cough medicines and many liquid vitamin preparations: Nyquil is 50 proof. Terpin Hydrate cough medicine can be as high as 80 proof, making it equivalent to gin, vodka, whiskey.
Antidepressants and stimulants such as: Elavil, Ritalin, amphetamine compounds.

Patterns

Weight control tablets.
Reserpine compounds, prescribed for hypertension, should be used with caution.

Disease of Alcoholism: Thirty Questions[11]

Please check the answer below that best describes your feelings, behavior and experiences related to a parent's alcohol use. Take your time and be as accurate as possible. Answer all thirty questions by checking either "Yes" or "No."

Yes	No	Questions
—	—	1. Have you ever thought that one of your parents had a drinking problem?
—	—	2. Have you ever lost sleep because of a parent's drinking?
—	—	3. Did you ever encourage one of your parents to quit drinking?
—	—	4. Did you ever feel alone, scared, nervous, angry, or frustrated because a parent was not able to stop drinking?
—	—	5. Did you ever argue or fight with a parent when he or she was drinking?
—	—	6. Did you ever threaten to run away from home because of a parent's drinking?
—	—	7. Has a parent ever yelled at or hit you or other family members when drinking?
—	—	8. Have you ever heard your parents fight when one of them was drunk?

—   —   9. Did you ever protect another family member from a parent who was drinking?

—   —   10. Did you ever feel like hiding or emptying a parent's bottle of liquor?

—   —   11. Do many of your thoughts revolve around a problem-drinking parent or difficulties that arise because of his or her drinking?

—   —   12. Did you ever wish that a parent would stop drinking?

—   —   13. Did you ever feel responsible for and guilty about a parent's drinking?

—   —   14. Did you ever fear that your parents would get divorced due to alcohol misuse?

—   —   15. Have you ever withdrawn from and avoided outside activities and friends because of embarrassment and shame over a parent's drinking problem?

—   —   16. Did you ever feel caught in the middle of an argument or fight between a problem-drinking parent and your other parent?

—   —   17. Did you ever feel that you made a parent drink alcohol?

—   —   18. Have you ever felt that a problem-drinking parent did not really love you?

—   —   19. Did you ever resent a parent's drinking?

—   —   20. Have you ever worried about a parent's health because of his or her alcohol use?

—   —   21. Have you ever been blamed for a parent's drinking?

—   —   22. Did you ever think your father was an alcoholic?

—   —   23. Did you ever wish your home could be more like the homes of your friends who did not have a parent with a drinking problem?

— — 24. Did a parent make promises to you that he or she did not keep because of drinking?

— — 25. Did you ever think your mother was an alcoholic?

— — 26. Did you ever wish you could talk to someone who could understand and help the alcohol-related problems in your family?

— — 27. Did you ever fight with your brothers/ sisters about a parent's drinking?

— — 28. Did you ever stay away from home to avoid the drinking parent or your other parent's reaction to the drinking?

— — 29. Have you ever felt sick, cried, or had a knot in your stomach after worrying about a parent's drinking?

— — 30. Did you ever take over any chores and duties at home that were usually done by a parent before he or she developed a drinking problem?

———— Total the number of "Yes" answers. A score of six or more means that more than likely this child is the child of an alcoholic parent.

Disease of Alcoholism: Twenty Questions[12]

Are you an alcoholic? Ask yourself the following questions and answer them as honestly as you can.

Yes	No	Questions
—	—	1. Do you lose time from work due to drinking?
—	—	2. Is drinking making your home life unhappy?
—	—	3. Do you drink because you are shy with other people?
—	—	4. Is drinking affecting your reputation?
—	—	5. Have you ever felt remorse after drinking?
—	—	6. Have you gotten into financial difficulties as a result of drinking?
—	—	7. Do you turn to lower companions and an inferior environment when drinking?
—	—	8. Does your drinking make you careless of your family's welfare?
—	—	9. Has your ambition decreased since drinking?
—	—	10. Do you crave a drink at a definite time daily?

—	—	11. Do you want a drink the next morning?
—	—	12. Does drinking cause you to have difficulty in sleeping?
—	—	13. Has your efficiency decreased since drinking?
—	—	14. Is drinking jeopardizing your job or business?
—	—	15. Do you drink to escape from worries or trouble?
—	—	16. Do you drink alone?
—	—	17. Have you ever had a complete loss of memory as a result of drinking?
—	—	18. Has your physician ever treated you for drinking?
—	—	19. Do you drink to build up your self-confidence?
—	—	20. Have you ever been to a hospital or institution on account of drinking?

If you answered "Yes" to any one of the questions, there is a definite warning that *you may be an alcoholic.*

If you answered "Yes" to any two, the chances are that you *are an alcoholic.*

If you answered "Yes" to three or more, *you are definitely an alcoholic.*

The above test questions and determinations are used by Johns Hopkins University Hospital, Baltimore, Maryland, in deciding whether or not a patient is alcoholic.

Appendix Five
Support Groups

Alcoholics Anonymous
P.O. Box 459
Grand Central Station
New York, NY 10163
(212) 686-1100
Also listed in your local phone book
I personally recommend closed—women only—meetings
for women.

Al-Anon/Alateen Family Group Headquarters, Inc.
P.O. Box 182
Madison Square Garden
New York, NY 10159
1-800-356-9996
Also listed in your local phone book

Adult Children of Alcoholics, Central Service Board
P.O. Box 35623
Los Angeles, CA 90035

(213) 464-4423
Also listed in your local phone book

Alcoholics for Christ, Inc.
1316 North Campbell Road
Royal Oak, MI 48067
Also may be listed in your local phone book

Alcoholics Victorious
May be listed in your local phone book

Lion Tamers Anonymous
First Evangelical Free Church
2801 North Brea Boulevard
Fullerton, CA 92635
(714) 529-5544

For complete information/locations, write:
U.S. Journal, Inc.
1721 Blount Road, Suite 1
Pompano Beach, Florida 33069
1-800-851-9100

APPENDIX SIX
TREATMENT CENTERS

These are just a few suggestions. For further information, write or call the following centers for their recommendations in your area, or write or call the U.S. Journal, Inc., as listed on previous page.

Springbrook
2001 Crestview Drive
Newberg, OR 97132
(503) 537-7000

Dunklin Memorial Camp
Route 1, Box 1600
Okeechobee, FL 33472
Combines the disease concept along with the emphasis on the higher power being that of Jesus Christ.

Hazeldon
P.O. Box 11
Center City, MN 55012-0011

Also provides the "I Do Care" intervention program.
In Minnesota: 1-800-257-0070
Out of state: 1-800-328-9000

Betty Ford Center
Eisenhower Hospital
P.O. Box 1560
Rancho Mirage, CA 92270
In California: 1-800-392-7540
Out of state: 1-800-854-9211

Endnotes

1. Antoine de Saint Exupery, The Little Prince (1943).
2. Norman Vincent Peale, The Power of Positive Thining (1952).
3. Norman Vincent Peale, The Positive Power of Jesus Christ (1980). Letter by author on pp. 63–65.
4. Charles Swindoll, Insight for Living publication.
5. Dr. Zuska, Sister Elizabeth Center, Orange, California.
6. Dr. David Olhms, The Disease Concept of Alcoholism video tape.
7. "Wellness Letter" (University of California–Berkeley: 1986).
8. James Milam, Ph.D. and Katherine Ketchum, Under The Influence.
9. John Crabbe, Oregonian (1992). Crabbe is researcher at Portland Veteran's Affairs Medical Center and professor of medical psychology at OHSU.
10. The Compulsive Woman by Sandra Simpson LeSourd, 1987.
11. J.W. Jones, Ph.D, "The Disease of Alcoholism 30 Questions."
12. Johns Hopkins University, "The Disease of Alcoholism 20 Questions."

To order additional copies of

PATTERNS

Have your credit card ready and call

Toll free: (877) 421-READ (7323)

or send $11.95* each plus $4.95 S&H**

to
WinePress Publishing
PO Box 428
Enumclaw, WA 98022

*Washington residents please add 8.4% tax.
**Add $1.00 S&H for each additional book ordered.